C000172255

SAN FRANCISCO

BY
NIGEL TISDALL

Produced by
Thomas Cook Publishing

CLOS PEGASE

Written by Nigel Tisdall
Updated by Maxine Cass
Photography by Ken Paterson and Maxine Cass
Original design by Laburnum Technologies Pvt Ltd

Editing and page layout by Cambridge Publishing
Management Ltd, Unit 2, Burr Elm Court,
Caldecote CB3 7NU
Series Editor: Karen Beaulah

Published by Thomas Cook Publishing
A division of Thomas Cook Tour Operations Ltd
Company Registration No. 1450464 England

PO Box 227, The Thomas Cook Business Park,
Unit 18, Coningsby Road,
Peterborough PE3 8SB, United Kingdom
E-mail: books@thomascook.com
www.thomascookpublishing.com
Tel: +44 (0)1733 416477

ISBN-13: 978-1-84157-705-0
ISBN-10: 1-84157-705-7

First edition © 2004 Thomas Cook Publishing
Second edition © 2006 Thomas Cook Publishing

Project Editor: Diane Ashmore
Production/DTP Editor: Steven Collins

Although every care has been taken in compiling this publication, and the contents are
believed to be correct at the time of printing, Thomas Cook Tour Operations Ltd cannot
accept any responsibility for errors or omissions, however caused, or for changes in details
given in the guidebook, or for the consequences of any reliance on the information provided.

The opinions and assessments expressed in this book do not necessarily represent those of
Thomas Cook Tour Operations Ltd.

Printed and bound in Spain by: Grafo Industrias Gráficas, Basauri.

Cover design by: Liz Lyons Design, Oxford.
Front cover credits: Left © Getty; centre © Chuck Pefley/Alamy; right © Workbook,
Inc/Photolibrary
Back cover credits: Left © Index Stock Imagery/Photolibrary; right © RonWatts/Corbis

Contents

KEY TO MAPS

✈ Airport

680 ① Road numbers

Ferry route

1022m ▲ Mountain

Cable car route

★ Start of walk/tour

☀ Viewpoint

ⓘ Information

Maps

Features

Walks and tours

Introduction

You hear such good things about San Francisco, it's bound to make a first-time visitor sceptical. Mention its name and invariably up pops a stock image of cable cars cruising a switchback of hills. In the background the fog is swirling around the Golden Gate Bridge, ferries are zipping across the Bay to Alcatraz, popcorn-munching children are laughing at the clowns on Fisherman's Wharf.

THOMAS COOK'S SAN FRANCISCO

Cook's Tours started business in America in 1865. Their first office in San Francisco opened ten years later. In 1876 a 'Personally-Conducted Tour of California' was launched, and the city became a regular port of call for the company's famous Round the World Tours.

Those shots in the tourist brochures don't lie, but neither do they give the whole picture. San Francisco is indeed a city heaven-made for a holiday – congenial, compact, walkable, with rewarding historical and cultural sights, a knock-out restaurant scene, hotels as grand as you fancy, and all the theatre, nightlife and sport you would expect of a major American city.

The views of San Francisco Bay from its panoramic hills are terrific, the weather is dramatic, there are vast, mature parks and long, romantic sands. Drive north across the soul-enhancing Golden Gate Bridge, head south down Highway 1, and you're immediately into scenic California, lost for choice between serene redwood forests, lonely shorelines and bucolic

wine valleys. Everything, in short, is here to guarantee San Francisco's position as one of the world's favourite holiday destinations.

But that's not what makes it so astonishingly popular, the sort of place where Tony Bennett could sing of leaving his heart and which sees new settlers arriving daily by plane, train, bus and car, looking for peace and the chance to kick a few dreams into place. For San Francisco is not so much a city as a phenomenon, a collective wish born in a gold rush, built on a fault line, framed by the bright blue Bay that was only discovered in 1769.

Optimists have been heading here for a century and a half now, rolling in like the Pacific fog that dances so famously through its skyscrapers.

In those pioneering days of tourism it took almost a week to travel from New York by railroad, and a berth in a sleeping car cost $22. The highlight of a visit to the city was a carriage drive in Golden Gate Park and an inspection of the seals at the Cliff House.

In 1915 the company was appointed Official Foreign Passenger Agent for the Panama-Pacific International Exposition, and from then on its business in the United States developed rapidly.

From the air the city looks as neat as computer circuitry: pockets of ornate Victorian housing, strips of seaside suburbia, boxed-up parks and question-mark freeways sweep up to a reach-for-the-sky Financial District bejewelled with Art Deco skyscrapers and mirror-glassed pomp.

Down on the streets the big sound is immigrant energy – an intoxicating cultural mixture with Italian, Chinese, Hispanic, Japanese and Southeast Asian neighbourhoods set in a spicy soup of diverse Californian lifestyles.

This is the city that gave us the Beats, hippy revolution, gay militancy and yuppies (a term first coined in the Bay Area). It doesn't mind where you sit on the gender rainbow, whether you like raves or Frank Sinatra, ballet or roller-blading, if you're here to lunch naked on the beach or take the kids to Alcatraz. Welcome to America's most tolerant city – it's one of the greatest in the world.

'You wouldn't think that such a place as San Francisco could exist. The wonderful sunlight there, the hills, the great bridges, the Pacific at your shoes. Beautiful Chinatown. Every race in the world.'
Dylan Thomas

Beautiful city: the view from Buena Vista Park to the Golden Gate Bridge and the Marin Headlands

The land

Bounded by the Pacific Ocean and the Bay, San Francisco stands at the northern tip of a peninsula formed by the Santa Cruz Mountains. The city covers 122sq km (47sq miles) and has approximately 745,000 citizens, making it one of the most densely populated cities in the United States.

San Francisco's distant skyline viewed from Fort Point

The Bay

San Francisco Bay is one of the best natural ports in America. Fed by 16 rivers, it covers 1,036sq km (400sq miles) and joins with the sea at the 5-km (3-mile) long strait of the Golden Gate. The Bay is actually a drowned river valley – its waters are 97m (318ft) deep beneath the Golden Gate Bridge but only 30.5m (100ft) under the eastern section of the Bay Bridge. Seventy per cent of it is less than 4m (12ft) deep.

Geology

San Francisco lies close to the San Andreas fault zone that runs the length of California and marks the division between the Pacific and North American tectonic plates. The Pacific Plate moves northwestward about 5cm (2in) every year, while the slower-moving North American Plate travels westward. The earthquake that devastated the city in 1906 was caused when subterranean pressures forced the Pacific Plate to suddenly leap forward 6m (20ft).

Landscape

San Francisco is draped across 43 hills, three of which – Twin Peaks, Mount Davidson and Mount Sutro – rise above 274m (900ft). Much of the city has been reclaimed from the Bayside shoreline, a process that began in 1849 when hundreds of ships were abandoned in the harbour by eager gold prospectors.

The beauty of the city owes much to its parks, in particular the 412-hectare (1,017-acre) Golden Gate Park which slices through the west of the city. Many other beaches, headlands and islands come under the jurisdiction of the Golden Gate National Recreation Area (GGNRA). In 1994 its natural empire benefited extensively from the addition of the 599-hectare (1,480-acre) Presidio,

OREGON
IDAHO
WYOMING
NEVADA
SAN FRANCISCO
CALIFORNIA
UTAH
Los Angeles
ARIZONA
PACIFIC OCEAN
MEXICO

one of the oldest military outposts in the United States.

Economy

Ever since the gold rush, San Francisco has been a city of service industries. From supplying prospectors with tools and then banking their gold, it developed into a thriving commercial and financial centre.

In the past, the port of San Francisco was kept busy with traditional sea-based industries such as fishing and shipbuilding. The port's fortunes were boosted by the opening of the Panama Canal in 1914 and by naval activity during World War II. Now it is in decline and its piers are increasingly given over to tourism – Pier 39 is a prime example. Visitors coming to the city on holiday or business have become a crucial component of San Francisco's economy, generating $6.7 billion from direct spending on tourism.

Bay Area

Seven million people live in the San Francisco metropolitan region, the fifth largest in the country. The area covers nine counties and extends north to the wine country of Napa and Sonoma, south to San Jose and Silicon Valley, and east to Alameda and Contra Costa Counties.

People

San Francisco and the Bay Area boast one of the most ethnically diverse communities in the United States. Around 56 per cent of the city's residents are non-white, while over one-third of San Franciscans are of Asian or Pacific background – a classic example of 'melting pot' America.

Twin Peaks Boulevard looking out over San Francisco skyline, San Francisco Bay, and East Bay hills

History

18,000 BC–AD 1500	Migrants from Asia cross the Bering Strait and populate the Americas. By the 16th century around 1½ million native Indians are spread across the United States, including 13,000 Miwoks and Ohlones in the Bay Area.
1579	Sailing up the Californian coast in the *Golden Hind*, Sir Francis Drake misses the entrance to San Francisco Bay. Landing at Drake's Bay in Marin County, he claims the land of Nova Albion for Queen Elizabeth I of England.
1769	Travelling overland, a Spanish expedition led by Gaspar de Portolá discovers the Bay of San Francisco. Over the next 54 years a string of 21 colonial missions is established between San Diego and Sonoma.
1775	The first ship sails into San Francisco Bay. Within a year the Spanish have founded the Presidio (fort) and a Mission named in honour of St Francis of Assisi.
1821	Mexico declares its independence from Spain

Barbary Coast Trail marker set in sidewalk in downtown San Francisco

	and encourages its citizens to settle in northern California.
1835	An English sea captain, William Richardson, founds the small town of Yerba Buena (Good Herb), which attracts an influx of American settlers.
1846	The United States declares war on Mexico. In Sonoma, the Bear Flag Revolt proclaims the short-lived (but long-remembered) independent republic of California. The USS *Portsmouth* sails into Yerba Buena, seizing the town for the Union and renaming it San Francisco.

1848	Gold is discovered 56km (35 miles) east of Sacramento. Thousands of prospectors rush to California, most through the port of San Francisco.		Coast. Seven years later the Southern Pacific Railroad connects it with Los Angeles. Construction is mostly carried out by immigrant Chinese labour.
1850	California becomes the 31st State of the Union with its capital in San Jose (it was later moved to Sacramento). Within two years the population has grown to 25,000.	**1870**	Founding of Golden Gate Park.
		1873	The world's first cable car trundles down Clay Street.
1869	The Central Pacific Railroad links San Francisco with the East	**1906**	An earthquake and ensuing fires devastate the city.

Murals from the 1915 Panama-Pacific Exposition

1915	The Panama-Pacific International Exposition celebrates the opening of the Panama Canal.
1933	Alcatraz Island becomes a Federal Penitentiary. Public works projects such as Coit Tower provide employment during the Great Depression.
1936–7	Opening of the Bay Bridge and the Golden Gate Bridge.
1939	Golden Gate International Exposition on Treasure Island attracts 17 million visitors.
1941–51	San Francisco becomes the hub of World War II military operations in the Pacific. In 1945 the original United Nations Charter is signed in the War Memorial Opera House and, in 1951, the Treaty marking the end of hostilities with Japan.
1950s	During the Cold War, San Francisco emerges as a haven for the Beat Generation, an artistic reaction to the conformity of post-war America.
1960s	In 1963 the prison on Alcatraz closes. In 1967 hippies fill the streets of Haight-Ashbury for the 'Summer of Love'. Protests against the US entry into the Vietnam War (1954–75) and campaigns for gay rights give the Bay Area a reputation as a centre of liberal activity.
1970s	In 1972 the Golden Gate National Recreation Area is created, and two years later the BART (Bay Area Rapid Transit) links San Francisco and Oakland. The Castro emerges as the centre of the city's growing gay community.
1989	An earthquake kills more than 60 people.
1990s	The Presidio joins the GGNRA and the 49ers win the Superbowl.
2000	Pacific Bell Park opens as the bayside home of San Francisco Giants.
2004	Almost 4,000 same-sex marriages at City Hall garner worldwide coverage.
2006	San Francisco bids to hold the 2016 Olympic Games.

Governance

Politics in San Francisco is never dull, and few visitors pass through the city without being at least warmed by the burning issues of the day.

To an outsider, San Francisco appears a deeply politicised city, a bastion of liberalism in a state where right-wing policies rule. It's not long before you meet a demo against Something Awful, or find the TV news dominated by Supervisor Scandal. Officially the city's political dramas are played out in the Civic Center, where the chief characters are the Mayor, who comes up for election every four years and has strong executive powers, and the 11-strong Board of Supervisors with whom legislative authority rests.

Politics in San Francisco means much more than voting for flag-waving parties. Issues of gender, race and the environment steal the front pages as often as crime and the economy do in other American cities. This is the town that gave us hippy freedoms and gay rights, where the cogs of the democratic process are openly displayed and Utopia

is being constructed by the Golden Gate. It's looking good so far, but visitors should know that it just isn't safe to walk the streets without carrying opinions – so get some quick, on vagrancy tickets for the homeless, draconian anti-smoking laws and 'three strikes and out' sentences for repeated offenders.

Emperor Norton I

The true story of Joshua A Norton typifies the buccaneering people politics of San Francisco. One day in 1859, after falling into sudden bankruptcy, this proud Anglo-South African merchant appeared in Montgomery Street wearing imperial military uniform. He informed the *San Francisco Bulletin* that he was the Emperor of the United States and Protector of Mexico. The city conspired to believe him for the next 21 years – minting a special Norton currency, printing his proclamations, and inviting the Emperor to top restaurants and theatrical first nights. When he died in 1880 thousands of loyal subjects attended his funeral.

City Hall is San Francisco's political stage

The gold rush

On 24 January 1848 James Marshall, a carpenter constructing a sawmill at Coloma, on the western slopes of the Sierra Nevada mountains, discovered nuggets of gold in the American River. His find triggered one of the most dramatic human migrations in history, and put San Francisco firmly on the world map.

Within a few months amateur prospectors were rushing to California in their thousands. Some travelled overland in wagon trains from the east coast, but the majority arrived by sea via Panama or the Cape Horn. In 1849, the year when the miners were christened 'Forty-niners', 40,000 optimists sailed into San Francisco Bay. Even the ships' crews rushed off to the gold fields, leaving the harbour at Yerba Buena clogged with numerous abandoned vessels that were incorporated into the rapidly growing town.

While a few struck it lucky, many fortune hunters fell victim to swindlers and profiteers. By the end of the 1850s, San Francisco had become a lawless boom town that fulfilled every Wild West cliché, an unromantic tale of saloons and whorehouses, gambling dens and vigilante gangs. According to *The Sacramento Union* newspaper, there were 1,400 murders in six years. The smart money, as ever, was in supply. Real and lasting fortunes were made by people like Levi Strauss, a hard-working German immigrant who arrived in 1853 and started kitting miners out with durable blue canvas trousers.

In 1859 silver was discovered in western Nevada, reviving San Francisco's role as a gateway to riches. By then

mining had become commercialised, creating a tycoon class that helped rebuild the city in grand style. Their large, ostentatious mansions crowned Nob Hill, which remains one of the most desirable

addresses in the city. Evocative mementoes of those pioneer times can be seen in the Wells Fargo History Museum (*see p97*).

The legacy of the gold rush has been far-reaching – from the gay community's supposed roots in the almost exclusively male population of the city 150 years ago, to businessmen who only half-joke that Wild West values persist in the Financial District. San Francisco is and always will be a city of fortune-seekers.

Prospectors who struck lucky (right) celebrated in the city's saloons (above) Facing page: Gold ore and gold coin, California State Mining and Mineral Museum, Mariposa

Culture

Your chances of meeting someone who can genuinely claim to be born, bred and still living in the midst of San Francisco are not good. This is 'a destination', where everyone comes from somewhere else and most genuine locals are either concentrated in ethnic neighbourhoods, or have defected to the suburbs and other Bay Area towns.

The music of the streets

As the North Beach poet Lawrence Ferlinghetti put it, San Francisco is where 'the frontier first got tamed'. The city is demographically unusual because the gold rush attracted two types of immigrants simultaneously – Americans racing overland from the East and ship-borne Europeans who had no experience of the Yankee way of doing things. Unlike the pioneer farmers and ranchers that traditionally settled the West, they came from all classes and backgrounds.

The result is a city of undying immigrant ambition, where brave new hopes are grafted on to cherished

Hispanic girls dressed for the Carnival, Mission District

memories of the old country. San Franciscans are justly proud of their multicultural diversity and tolerance of other people's lifestyles, and exude a spirit of getting along that other cities probably only enjoy in times of war. And, perhaps because the Big 'Quake could happen at any moment, they never forget that life is about having a good time.

Art
The opening of the San Francisco Museum of Modern Art in a modern venue in 1995 confirmed the city's credentials as the art capital of the West. Its cultural pedigree stretches back to 1871 and the founding of the San Francisco Art Institute, now located in Chestnut Street, which has played an influential role in the development of art in the Bay Area. Many of the city's commercial galleries can be found close to the Financial District in Sutter and Post streets and Grant Avenue.

Music and dance
San Francisco's first opera house opened in 1851, and the present War Memorial Opera House in Civic Center was the first municipally owned venue in

America. Both the San Francisco Opera and the San Francisco Symphony have a high reputation, while the San Francisco Ballet is the oldest professional company in the United States. There is also a vigorous interest in modern and ethnic dance and music.

The city will always be known for the Sixties sounds that became a backing track for the hippy revolution. Legendary performers like Janis Joplin, Jefferson Airplane and The Grateful Dead played Golden Gate Park and the Fillmore Auditorium. The Bill Graham Civic Auditorium in the Civic Center pays tribute to the promoter who virtually invented the modern rock concert. San Franciscans also have a penchant for enjoying big feelings in small clubs – jazz and blues both flourished in North Beach venues and now inspire respected annual festivals, while SOMA (the area South of Market Street) is renowned for its hip dance clubs.

Education

The intellectual life of the Bay Area has always been dominated by the world-class universities at Stanford and Berkeley. Their academic achievements, sporting rivalry and shared history of student activism have tended to obscure San Francisco's own educational institutions.

The oldest of these is the University of San Francisco, located near the northeast corner of Golden Gate Park Panhandle. Founded in 1855 and still run by Jesuits, the twin towers of its St Ignatius Church are a familiar landmark in the west of the city. Further south near Mount Sutro, the University of California, San Francisco dates from 1899 and is known in particular for its medical research.

Murals in the Mission: street paintings are a commentary on life in San Francisco

Writers and poets

I do not know,' Anthony Trollope declared in 1875, 'that in all my travels I visited a city less interesting.' Whatever writers have to say about San Francisco, it is rarely bland. The city has inspired a feast of novels, poetry and high-octane journalism that provides an engrossing chronicle of its moods and moments.

Like the early San Franciscans, many authors were roving fortune hunters themselves. Mark Twain (1835–1910) moved to the city in 1864 after a fruitless stab at gold prospecting (recalled in *Roughing It*), while the love of a married woman brought an impecunious Robert Louis Stevenson (1850–94) to a garret in Bush Street in 1879. Jack London (1876–1916), who was born in San Francisco but moved to Oakland at age three, dropped out of UC Berkeley to join the Klondike gold rush, and concluded a life of volatile wandering by building a home in Glen Ellen, Sonoma. Amongst his frenetic output is a gripping eyewitness account of the 1906 earthquake.

San Francisco life is also recorded in depth in works by Frank Norris (1870–1902) and Ambrose Bierce (1842–1914), who both worked for local newspapers, while Dashiell

JACK KEROUAC STREET

On January 25, 1988
The City of San Francisco
approved a proposal by
CITY LIGHTS BOOKS
to rename 12 streets for
S.F. writers and artists
including this alley.

Hammett (1894–1961), the guru of hard-boiled detective fiction, lived in the city centre for most of the 1920s. He can be held responsible for the city's image as a badly lit playground for back-alley sleuths – the first Sam Spade novel, *The Maltese Falcon*, was completed in 1929.

In the 1950s, as writers like Jack Kerouac and Allen Ginsberg challenged literary and social orthodoxies, San Francisco developed a reputation as America's Poetry Corner. Lawrence Ferlinghetti opened the City Lights Bookstore in North Beach, Ginsberg read *Howl* and the Beat Generation was born. The following decade saw San Francisco become the centre of the hippy world, and its drug-fuelled highs and lows were vividly chronicled by writers like Tom Wolfe and Hunter S Thompson.

More recently, Armistead Maupin's *Tales from the City*, Vikram Seth's epic narrative poem *The Golden Gate*, and the novels of American-Chinese authors Amy Tan and Maxine Hong Kingston, have continued the story of San Francisco.

Facing page: Signage at Jack Kerouac Street
Above: Façade of City Lights Bookstore, San Francisco

Impressions

'It's an odd thing, but anyone who disappears is said to have been seen in San Francisco. It must be a delightful city and possess all the attractions of the next world.'

OSCAR WILDE
1882

Orientation

San Francisco is built on a grid pattern of streets that takes little notice of the major hills underneath. The two widest streets sit on the map like a pair of dividers and will soon become familiar – the diagonal Market Street and the north–south Van Ness Avenue. Most hotels, and popular areas such as the Financial District, North Beach and Fisherman's Wharf, lie within the northeast quadrant of the city enclosed by these streets. The surrounding neighbourhoods and parks have much to offer, too – for a perfect introduction to the complete city follow the 49-Mile Scenic Drive (*see p104*).

Ten things a stranger should know
- drive on the right
- the first floor is the ground floor
- only gauche out-of-towners call it 'Frisco'
- buffalo wings are spicy chicken wings
- you won't get high on hash browns
- jelly is jam and jello is jelly
- a rubber is a condom not an eraser
- a sub isn't a loan but a filled long roll
- never say 'nice trolley' to a cable-car gripman
- the customer knows best, so pretend you do

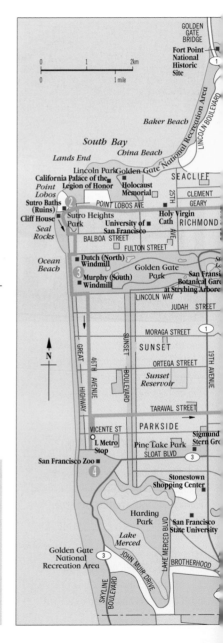

San Francisco (*see p100 for orange route bus tour*)

first steps

Cable cars are not only a tourist attraction but a fun way to travel round the city

Arriving

Most visitors arrive by air at San
Francisco International Airport (SFO),
22.5km (14 miles) south of the city
centre. A shuttle bus is the quickest
way to get to your accommodation –
the journey takes about 30 minutes,
though rush hour could make it longer
(*see p176*).

Getting around
Public transport
511®

For up-to-date
information on
San Francisco
Bay Area
transportation,
visit *www.511.org*,
or call 511 for

Combined MUNI
and BART stops

one-stop public transport and bicycle
route maps, traffic reports and
schedules.

Cable cars are a city trademark.
The two most popular lines of San
Francisco's three cable-car routes
(*see pp54–5*), Powell/Hyde and
Powell/Mason, start from a turntable
by Hallidie Plaza, at the junction of
Powell and Market streets. At peak
times there can be long queues. Your
chances won't improve by walking up
to the next stop, so tough it out with the
buskers or adopt an alternative strategy
– such as riding the cars early in the
morning, in the evening, or taking the
less-crowded California Street line
(*see pp24–5*).

MUNI (San Francisco Municipal
Railway) operates a complex but
comprehensive public transport network
reaching all corners of the city. It is
worth befriending the bus system, as

this is a cheap and reliable way to enjoy San Francisco (*see p100* for a suggested ride). In addition, there are five MUNI metro lines with streetcars that run underground in the city centre and on the surface in outlying parts. Historic streetcars from around the world run on the F line.

Travel on MUNI is efficient but impersonal – a bus ride is $1.50 (children 50¢) and drivers don't give change. It will probably be economical to buy a MUNI Passport, valid for 1, 3 or 7 days, which allows unlimited travel on buses, metro lines and cable cars, as well as offering discounted admission to some museums and sights. These can be bought online, at SFO information booths and other outlets, along with the useful MUNI Street and Transit Map. Find MUNI routes for major tourist attractions online at *www.sfmuni.com/cms/mms/ rider/visitors.htm*. CityPass offers 7 days of cable car, bus and streetcar transportation, a bay cruise and multiple museum admissions at discount.

BART (Bay Area Rapid Transit) provides speedy access by rail around the Bay Area including service to SFO airport, and has some shared stops with the MUNI metro stations in Market Street.

Ferry services are geared to the needs of commuters as well as tourists, and are an exhilarating way to enjoy San Francisco Bay (*see p130*).

Taxis are reasonably priced and ubiquitous except when it's raining, cold or you need one in a hurry. Hotels are the best place to start looking – at night book one by phone rather than hang around in the street. An illuminated roof-sign indicates a taxi is accepting passengers.

For public transport maps and further information *see pp183–6*.

Driving

You don't need a car to see the city's main sights – buses, cable cars and taxis can get you anywhere. However, the use of a vehicle for a few days will allow you to follow the 49-Mile Drive and take day trips to Muir Woods, the Napa and Sonoma wine valleys or tour the Bay. When planning journeys try to avoid the weekday rush hours between 6.30am and 9.30am, and 3pm and 6pm. *www.511.org*

MUNI information
Tel: (415) 673 6864; www.sfmuni.com
San Francisco CityPass
www.citypass.com/city/sanfrancisco.html
BART information
Tel: (415) 989 2278; www.bart.gov
Yellow Cab Cooperative
Tel: (415) 333 3333; www.yellowcabsf.com

Buses are a cheap and easy way to get around

Golden Gate Bridge veiled by fog, seen from south side near Fort Point

Fog

The city's souvenir shops make a nice few bucks selling 'I Love San Francisco' sweatshirts to visitors unprepared for the chill mornings of 'Fog City'. The rest of California might well be full of sun-drenched beaches and fire hazard warnings, but San Francisco has its own exhibitionist microclimate in summer that brings fog racing through the Golden Gate Bridge like dry ice. Don't be put off: the fog is great fun, a mystical, comforting character that rolls in for a morning chat but has often vanished by mid-afternoon.

Safety

Major earthquakes in 1906 and 1989 (*see pp56–7*) are a reminder that San Francisco is built on a fault line. Many new buildings have been constructed to withstand tremors, while older ones carry solemn warnings implying that you are about to shop in a rickety pack of cards, so don't even think about post-earthquake litigation. If the earth moves, the official advice is to seek cover, move away from windows, don't use lifts, and don't run outside.

As in all large American cities, crime and potentially hostile street characters are a problem. Avoid all parks and deserted or poorly lit streets at night, carry no ostentatious valuables and leave nothing you care about in a car. Tourists should avoid straying into the Tenderloin, a rough and depressed area west of Union Square and north of the Civic Center, bounded loosely by O'Farrell, Polk, Mason and Market Streets. Panhandlers are obvious and sometimes aggressive, particularly near Union Square and along Market Street. Most San Franciscans decline politely and continue on their way.

Smoking

As the result of prohibitionary legislation, smokers are made to feel as welcome in San Francisco as lepers at a medieval fair. One of the bizarre Financial District sights is the designer-dressed, chain-puffing executives who gather outside the entrances to their smoking-free palaces like naughty schoolkids – a delinquent assembly that has now prompted signs declaring 'No Smoking within 15 feet of this building'. The message is clear – if you are a smoker, go outside to light up. It is illegal to smoke in bars, restaurants, shops, offices, modes of transport and public areas including parks. All hotels now have non-smoking rooms and floors. Many are smoke-free. Make your needs known when you make a reservation.

Tourist information
The helpful San Francisco Visitor Information Center is on the lower level of Hallidie Plaza, by the junction of Powell and Market streets and the Powell Street MUNI/BART station. *Tel: (415) 391 2000; www. onlyinsanfrancisco.com. Events Information tel: (415) 391 2001. Open: Mon–Fri 9am–5pm, weekends & holidays 9am–3pm.*

Money-saving tips
- Buy a MUNI Passport or CityPass for travel (*see p21*).
- Some museums and the Japanese Tea Garden offer a discount with a MUNI transfer.
- Buy half-price theatre tickets from the TIX Bay Area kiosk in Union Square (*see p142*).
- Portions in restaurants are often large, so don't order more than you need. You can take away what's left in a 'doggy bag'.
- Free-of-charge San Francisco sights include the Cable Car Barn, Fort Point, Golden Gate Bridge, the Maritime Museum, plus vibrant neighbourhoods like Chinatown, North Beach and the Mission.
- The free, volunteer-led walks organised by The Friends of San Francisco Library cover many historical and cultural aspects of the city. Donations accepted (*see pp28–9*).
- Some museums offer free admission one day in each month.
  Tuesday – Asian Art Museum, California Palace of the Legion of Honor, de Young Museum, SFMOMA, Yerba Buena Center for the Arts.
  Wednesday – California Academy of Sciences, Exploratorium.
  Saturday – Bay Area Discovery Museum. (*See individual entries for exact times.*)

The busy San Francisco Visitor Information Center in Hallidie Plaza, near the MUNI/BART station and cable-car turnaround

Cable cars

Devised in 1873 by a Scottish engineer, Andrew Hallidie, San Francisco's world-famous cable-car system has survived earthquakes, fires and decades of neglect to become a much-loved tourist attraction that is also a great way to get around.

A wire manufacturer and designer of haulage systems for the gold mines, Hallidie is said to have been spurred to invention after witnessing an accident in which several horses died after their well-laden carriage dragged them back down a steep hill. His first cars, one of which can be seen in the Cable Car Barn and Museum (see p36), ran along Clay Street. The following year eight more lines were built and put into service, and by the end of the decade the network covered 180km (112 miles).

Cable cars operate by gripping on to a continuously moving woven steel cable set in the centre of the street, which runs in a loop powered from the Cable Car Barn in Mason Street. A gripman in the centre of the car uses a pliers-like lever to control the movement of the car, which runs at an average 15kph (9.5mph).

In the early 1980s the entire cable-car system was overhauled at a cost of $67 million. Of the three lines in operation, the most popular are Powell/Mason and Powell/Hyde, which use one-way cars with a turntable at either end. The quieter California Street line uses cars with a driver's cab at each end. Each car has a two-person crew who can be as colourful and temperamental as their equipment.

Though at times San Francisco's cable cars can become over-crowded tourist traps, they are still used by locals (who are adept queue-jumpers) and provide an irresistible source of inexpensive fairground thrills. Hopping on a vintage wooden car at sunset is like buying a ticket back to city life a century ago.

Who could fail to enjoy that lurching whoosh as you charge down to Fisherman's Wharf with the gripman banging his bell as if the Apocalypse was nigh? Was public transport ever so much fun?

Facing page: California Line cable car in front of Old St Mary's Cathedral, Chinatown
Top: Powell Mason Line cable car turning from Jackson Street on to Mason Street
Above: original cable car from the Clay Street Hill Railway at the Cable Car Museum (period photographs show it in service)

Neighbourhoods

San Francisco is a city of diverse neighbourhoods, and the opportunity to plunge into many different worlds in the space of a bus ride is a fundamental part of its appeal to both residents and visitors. Neighbourhood borders are imprecise, fluctuating with the processes of gentrification and ethnic drift that move through the city, but the following areas all have a tangible identity.

City centre

The heart of San Francisco is often referred to as simply Downtown, and the majority of the city's shops, offices, theatres and hotels can be found in the grid of streets surrounding Union Square. This is the area where most visitors stay. To its east rise the skyscrapers of the Financial District, and to its west lies the seedy Tenderloin, now home to a growing Southeast Asian community. The Beaux-Arts public buildings of the Civic Center fill the corner between Market Street and Van Ness Avenue. The streets to the west of Van Ness Avenue are known as the Western Addition, a mix of historic Victorian housing, severe modern estates and Japantown, the colourful focus of San Francisco's Japanese community.

Boulevard in Sunset: San Francisco is a city of many characterful neighbourhoods

Neighbourhoods

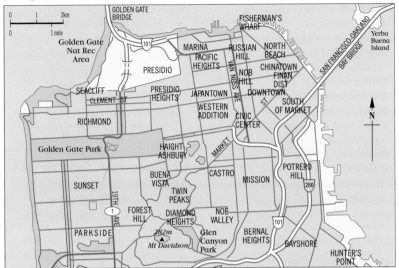

Northeast

To the north of Downtown lie the busy streets of Chinatown, the traditional home of San Francisco's Chinese-American citizens. This is bordered by North Beach, an historic Italian neighbourhood with abundant cafés and restaurants. Its main street, Columbus Avenue, is overlooked to the east by Coit Tower-capped Telegraph Hill, and to the west by Russian Hill, a smart residential district. Even more exclusive is nearby Nob Hill, its summit crowned with grand hotels and millionaire mansions since the 1880s. The piers of Fisherman's Wharf surround San Francisco's northeast shore – once devoted to fishing boats and ferries, but now overwhelmed by the tourist trade.

South of Market Street (SOMA)

As well as being a main transport artery leading to the Ferry Building, Market Street is a traditional socio-economic dividing line that signals cultural change. Once an area of light industry and warehousing, SOMA (the area South of Market Street) is becoming gentrified, most noticeably around the arts centre of Yerba Buena Gardens and at the area's east end, where waterfront buildings along The Embarcadero and South Beach have been restored. South of 16th Street, the Mission District is the long-standing home of San Francisco's Hispanic population, while the city's gay community is centred on the Castro. Further south lie two predominantly working-class neighbourhoods, Potrero Hill and Noe Valley.

West

The Marina District, tucked between Fort Mason and the Presidio, is a sports-conscious sidekick of Pacific Heights,

San Francisco's premier family neighbourhood, with smart schools, yuppie-packed restaurants and nonstop shopping in Union Street.

The Richmond District, sandwiched between the Presidio and Golden Gate Park, is a residential belt of staid, middle-class housing that stretches to Ocean Beach, with Clement Street as a second Chinatown. Its conservative refrains are picked up to the south in the Sunset District.

By contrast, the Haight-Ashbury, gathered around the Panhandle of Golden Gate Park, has been resolutely alternative since it became famous as a hippy mecca in the Sixties. Towards the south, the houses hugging the steep slopes of Twin Peaks enjoy the best views of the city.

Walks

The many guided walking tours of San Francisco's neighbourhoods are highly recommended. Led by locals who know their area inside out, they often include a meal or drink at venues you would never find on your own, and are the best way for a stranger to gain a rapid insight into the city.

San Francisco City guides

Cultural walks on many themes organised by the Friends of San Francisco Public Library, including mural tours of the Mission. *Tel: (415) 557 4266; www.sfcityguides.org Free admission but donations accepted.*

Walking tours of neighbourhoods are usually informative and fun

Cruisin' the Castro
A stroll through San Francisco's gay community.
Tel: (415) 255 1821;
www.cruisinthecastro.com

Dashiell Hammett Tour
Visit the most famous haunts of Sam Spade, San Francisco's best-known detective, and the writer who brought him to life. Your guide sports a trenchcoat and snap-brim hat.
www.donherron.com

FOOT!
Comedians walk and joke through several hours of Haight-Ashbury *Flashback*, *Hobnobbing with Gobs of Snobs* (Nob Hill), *Chasing the Dragon* (Chinatown), and more.
Tel: (415) 793 5378; www.foottours.com

Stairways across San Francisco
Keep in shape while on holiday, with nonstop walking tour routes that wind through neighbourhoods over challenging hills, via more than 100 stairways.
Tel: (415) 261 0813;
www.perfectsites.com/Stairways/

Wok Wiz
Walks around Chinatown with the option of a *dim-sum* lunch.
Tel: (415) 981 8989; www.wokwiz.com

Vampire Tour
A night-time tour of Nob Hill and the vampires who (may have) dined there.
Tel: (650) 279 1840; (866) 424 8836;
www.sfvampiretour.com

Victorian Home Walk
Everything about San Francisco's elegant Victorian buildings.
Tel: (415) 252 9485;
www.victorianwalk.com

Tours
Guided tours of the city by small bus or motorised cable car, and Bay Area excursions with a ferry ride or cruise, are offered by many companies.

A Day in Nature
Walks in Muir Woods, Marin and Napa with picnic. Maximum of five.
Tel: (415) 673 0548;
www.adayinnature.com

A Friend in Town
Personal tours of San Francisco, Oakland, Berkeley, Muir Woods, Wine Country, Silicon Valley and other areas around the Bay by private minivan.
Tel: (800) 960 8099;
www.toursanfranciscobay.com

Cable Car Charters
Narrated tours by motorised cable car.
Tel: (415) 922 2425; (800) 562 7283;
www.cablecarcharters.com.

Gray Line/San Francisco Sightseeing and Tours
Choice of over 20 tours, including city tours, visits to Muir Woods and the Wine Country, Bay cruises.
Tel: (415) 434 8687; (888) 428 6937;
www.graylinesanfrancisco.com

For scenic flights and boat trips *see p128 & p130.*

City centre (*see p54 for orange route tour*)

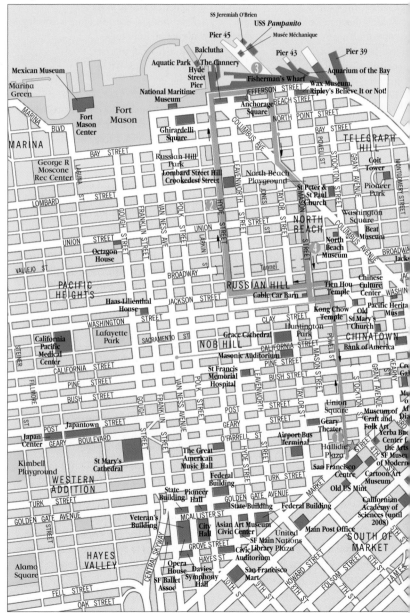

SS Jeremiah O'Brien
USS *Pampanito*
Pier 45
Musée Méchanique
Balclutha
Pier 43
Pier 39
Aquatic Park   The Cannery
Aquarium of the Bay
Mexican Museum
Hyde
Street
Pier
Aquatic Park
Fisherman's Wharf   Wax Museum,
Ripley's Believe It or Not!
Marina
Green
National Maritime
Museum
JEFFERSON   STREET
Fort
Mason Center
Fort
Mason
Anchorage
Square
BEACH STREET
NORTH POINT STREET
Ghirardelli
Square
COLUMBUS AVE
BAY   STREET
TELEGRAPH
HILL
MARINA
BAY   STREET
POWELL
STOCKTON
GRANT   AVENUE
MONTGOMERY STREET
George R
Moscone
Rec Center
Russian Hill
Park
Lombard Street Hill
Crookedest Street
North Beach
Playground
Coit
Tower
Pioneer
Park
LOMBARD   ST
STREET
FRANKLIN
VAN   NESS   AVE
POLK
LARKIN
LEAVENWORTH
HYDE
JONES
TAYLOR
MASON
St Peter &
St Paul
Church
Washington
Square
Beat
Museum
UNION
GOUGH
STREET
STREET
UNION   STREET
STREET
STREET
NORTH
BEACH
North
Beach
Museum
COLUMBUS   AVENUE
Octagon
House
BROADWAY
BROADWAY
Tunnel
Jack
VALLEJO   ST
PACIFIC
HEIGHTS
RUSSIAN HILL
Cable Car Barn
Chinese
Culture
Center
WASHIN
Haas-Lilienthal
House
JACKSON   STREET
Tien Hou
Temple
Pacific Herita
Mus
WASHINGTON
STREET
CLAY   STREET
Kong Chow
Temple
Old
St Mary's
Church
California
Pacific
Medical
Center
Lafayette
Park
SACRAMENTO   ST
NOB HILL
Grace Cathedral
Huntington
Park
CHINATOWN
STEINER
CALIFORNIA STREET
Masonic Auditorium
CALIFORNIA   STREET
Bank of America
FILLMORE
PINE   STREET
PINE STREET
St Francis
Memorial
Hospital
BUSH STREET
POWELL ST
KEARNY
Cre
Gal
BUSH   STREET
VAN NESS AVENUE
POLK
FRANKLIN
GOUGH
LEAVENWORTH
TAYLOR
MASON
STOCKTON
GRANT   AVENUE
Mu
o
M
Dia
POST
Japantown   STREET
STREET
POST   STREET
Union
Square
Museum of
Craft and
Folk Art
Japan
Center
GEARY   BOULEVARD
GEARY
STREET
Geary
Theater
Yerba Bue
Center f
the Arts
Kimball
Playground
St Mary's
Cathedral
O'FARRELL   ST
Airport Bus
Terminal
Hallidie
Plaza
SF Museum
of Modern
WESTERN
ADDITION
The Great
American
Music Hall
HYDE   ST
San Francisco
Centre
Cartoon Art
Museum
Federal
Building
TURK   STREET
Old US Mint
TURK   STREET
State
Building
Pioneer
Hall
GOLDEN GATE AVENUE
MARKET
Californian
Academy of
Sciences (until
2008)
GOLDEN GATE   AVENUE
State Building
Federal Building
Main Post Office
SOUTH OF
MARKET
CENTRAL SKYWAY
Veteran's
Building
MCALLISTER ST
City
Hall
Asian Art Museum
Civic Center
United
Nations
SF Main
Library Plaza
HAYES   STREET
GROVE   STREET
Civic
Auditorium
HOWARD STREET
HAYES
VALLEY
Opera
House   Davies
Symphony
Hall
San Francisco
Mart
FOLSOM   ST
Alamo
Square
SF Ballet
Assoc
FELL   STREET
OAK   STREET

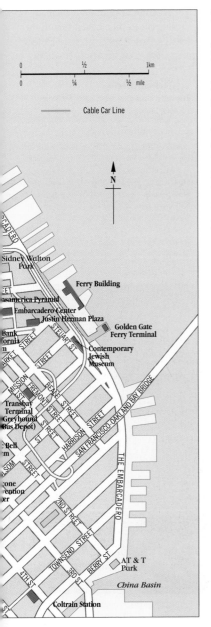

0   ½   1km

0   ¼   ½ mile

——— Cable Car Line

N

Sidney Walton Park

Ferry Building

...samerica Pyramid

Embarcadero Center

Justin Herman Plaza

Bank ...ornia ...n

Golden Gate Ferry Terminal

Contemporary Jewish Museum

Transbay Terminal Greyhound Bus Depot

...Bell ...m

...one ...ention ...er

AT & T Park

China Basin

Coltrain Station

San Francisco

Alcatraz

Between 1934 and 1963 the 9-hectare (22-acre) rocky island of Alcatraz was home to the most notorious male prison in America, incarcerating legendary criminals such as Al Capone, 'Machine Gun' Kelly and Robert Stroud, who was canonised by Hollywood as the 'Birdman of Alcatraz'. Its name comes from the pelicans (*alcatraces* in Spanish) that perch on its cliffs and rocks – for all its grim history, the island has also served as a wildlife sanctuary attracting brown pelicans, night herons, western gulls and many other birds.

Alcatraz was first fortified in 1859 by the US Army, and until 1933 served as a military prison. Barracks, casemates (gun positions), the guardhouse, a chapel and parade ground linger from

San Francisco in Quicktime

If you only have a short time in San Francisco, a priority sightseeing list might include:

- a cable-car ride (*see pp54–5*)
- dinner in North Beach (*see p162*)
- a boat trip to Alcatraz or Sausalito (*see p130*)
- a visit to the San Francisco Museum of Modern Art (*see p90*)
- a walk or cycle ride across the Golden Gate Bridge (*see pp60–61 & pp102–3*)
- shopping in Chinatown (*see p44*)
- climbing to the top of Coit Tower (*see p92*)
- taking the kids to the Exploratorium (*see p52*)
- a visit to the Golden Gate Park (*pp62–3*)
- inspecting the historic ships at Hyde Street Pier (*see p70*)
- driving the 49-Mile Scenic Drive (*see pp104–5*).

this period. Some of the later buildings used by the Federal Penitentiary staff are now in ruins, such as the Warden's House and Post Exchange (then used as a shop and sports hall).

After the closure of the penitentiary in 1963, the island was occupied between 1969 and 1971 by American Indians campaigning for native rights. Fires and vandalism destroyed some buildings, though faded graffiti can still be seen in places. Since 1972 Alcatraz has been amalgamated as part of the Golden Gate National Recreation Area.

Exploring Alcatraz

The crossing to the island takes 15 minutes. Visitors can stay as long as the ferry schedules permit, but there are no refreshment or picnic facilities on the island. A Park Ranger greets each ferry and provides information. If you like to

Escape from Alcatraz

The 14 recorded escape attempts from Alcatraz range from the brutal to the ingenious. Some prisoners were shot dead by guards, others were found hiding on the island, and many were frustrated by the icy waters of the Bay. In 1945 John Giles, who worked in the prison laundry, reached San Francisco disguised in military uniform but was immediately recaptured. No prisoner is known to have got off the island alive, though five are still missing. On the last attempt in 1962, John Paul Scott managed to swim to rocks beside the Golden Gate Bridge, but was too exhausted to get further.

The scenic location of Alcatraz Island belies the brutal history of its prison

A cell block on Alcatraz Island, Golden Gate National Recreation Area

enjoy the island at your own pace, a brochure with a self-guiding trail is available and there are ranger-led tours on themes such as natural history and escape attempts, as well as the Native American presence.

Cellhouse

Beginning in late 2006, you start the tour at the shower rooms, following the path of newly arrived convicts, before entering the cell blocks. A 35-minute self-guided audio tour using the voices of former inmates and prison officers brings to life the cell blocks and living quarters. Corridors were given ironic nicknames like 'Broadway', 'Times Square' and 'Seedy Street', and the violent activities of the 250 convicts provided rich material for the writers of headlines and film scripts. An exhibit in one cell shows how three of them, Frank Lee Morris and the Anglin brothers, attempted to escape by digging through their walls and leaving dummy heads in bed to fool prison staff. Visitors can also see the dining hall, recreation yard and prison gardens.

GGNRA Alcatraz information:
Tel: (415) 561 4900, (415) 705 1042;
www.nps.gov/alcatraz
In summer the first boat leaves at 9.30am, the last returns at 6.30pm. Two-hour Alcatraz Evening Tours offer a quick overview of the cell block and facilities. Free admission to the island but there is a charge for the ferry and optional audio tour. Advance booking by credit card is strongly recommended to avoid a lengthy wait. Ferry: Blue & Gold Fleet from Pier 41. Tel: (415) 705 5555;
www.blueandgoldfleet.com. From Sept 21 2006, ferries will be operated by Alcatraz Cruises. Tel: (415) 981 7625;
www.alcatrazcruises.com

Interpretive sign about 'The Battle of Alcatraz' in 1946

Interior of the Asian Art Museum, Civic Center (former Public Library building)

Alamo Square

A showcase for the city's Victorian mansions, this grassy hilltop offers one of the most photographed scenic views of the city. Steiner Street, on its east side, is a bright

Asian Art Museum sculpture

cascade of Queen Anne 'painted ladies' (*see pp84–5*), including a splendid buttermilk madam at No. 850. In vivid contrast, behind this 'Postcard Row' soar the skyscraping tower blocks of the Financial District raised a century later.

Set aside as a park in 1856, this historic district developed quickly in the 1890s and has an appealing architectural unity. The neighbourhood to the north is known as the Western Addition from the planned westward expansion of the city that took place in the last quarter of the 19th century. Settled by the Japanese and then African-American communities, many of its Victorian buildings were demolished in the 1960s and replaced by grim housing projects. *Bus: 21. Avoid the park at night.*

Aquarium of the Bay

Adjacent to Pier 39, this aquarium supplements the usual tanks of creatures with 23,000 aquatic denizens, swimming in the vicinity of two clear tunnels that you transit on a moving walkway. After seeing San Francisco Bay, a 'Touch the Bay' area recreates a coastal reef, with tide pools and touch pools containing bat rays and leopard sharks.

Pier 39, Embarcadero at Beach Street. Tel: (888) 732 3483, (415) 623 5300; www.aquariumofthebay.com. Open: Mon–Fri 10am–6pm, Sat–Sun 10am–7pm (longer in summer). Admission charge. Muni: F-line. Bus: 10, 39 & 47.

Bay cruises

The best way to see San Francisco Bay is from the water. The budget version is a commuter ferry ride from the Ferry Building at the foot of Market Street. Travellers with more time or cash should head for Pier 39 and Fisherman's Wharf. Blue & Gold Fleet tours circle beneath the Bay Bridge and the Golden Gate Bridge with views of Alcatraz, Angel Island, Treasure Island and the San Francisco waterfront. Red and White Fleet tours visit Alcatraz, Angel Island and other points.

Blue & Gold Fleet *Pier 41 Marine Terminal, just east of Pier 39. Tel: (415) 705 5555; www.blueandgoldfleet.com Cruises daily.*
Red and White Fleet *Pier 43. 1/2 Fisherman's Wharf. Tel: (415) 673 2900, (415) 901 5254; www.redandwhite.com Cruises daily.*

The 'Postcard Row' of Victorian mansions in Alamo Square is a landmark of city architecture

Aquatic Park

At the west end of Fisherman's Wharf, this small beach and park was created in the 1930s and is a microcosm of San Francisco. Tourists come for its historic ships, cable cars and the shops of Ghirardelli Square. You're likely to encounter a number of crafts stalls, kite fliers, paddling children, sand-sculpting panhandlers and hippies chanting to the sunset. Walk around its curling pier, always popular with crab fishermen, to look back at a great view of the city.

Beach St at Polk St.
Cable car: Powell/Hyde. Bus: 19 & 30.

Beat Museum

Beat Generation photos, letters, a once-confiscated edition of poet Allen Ginsberg's *Howl*, and other artefacts. The museum recently moved to the neighbourhood where author Jack Kerouac characterised a week in San Francisco as the 'beatest' of his life.

1345 Grant Ave. Tel: (800) 537 6822;
www.thebeatmuseum.org. Open: Tue–Sun
10am–8pm. Closed: Mon. Free admission.
Bus: 15, 30, 41.

Cable Car Barn and Museum

An integral part of San Franciscan life and lore, cable cars have been running in the city since 1873 (*see p24*). At the heart of the network is a red-brick building just west of Chinatown, where the singing cables wind round huge sheaves. Built in 1909 as the Ferry and Cliffhouse Railways Powerhouse, the Cable Car Barn is still used as a maintenance and control centre, but now also doubles as a working museum explaining the history and inner mysteries of this unique system.

Downstairs in the oily Sheave Room, a viewing area enables visitors to see the great drum wheels turning beneath the intersection of Mason and Washington Streets. Upstairs, a second viewing platform overlooks the beautiful spinning wheels powering the woven steel cables, which must have made a pretty picture of Victorian industry in the days of steam. The cables have to be replaced at least once a year, a task carried out overnight.

The adjacent area is filled with several historic cable cars, including one from Hallidie's original 1873 fleet. Its survival is something of a miracle, as it was on loan for an exhibition in Baltimore when the 1906 earthquake struck San Francisco. The following year that city was struck by a great fire, but the car escaped damage and was subsequently discovered in 1939 lingering in a local junkyard. A shop sells books and souvenirs, while display panels and a video tell the story of San Francisco's cable cars.

Washington St at 1201 Mason St.
Tel: (415) 474 1887;
www.cablecarmuseum.org
Open: daily 10am–6pm (till 5pm
Oct–Mar). Free admission.
Cable car: Powell/Mason, Powell/Hyde.

California Academy of Sciences

When the oldest natural history museum in the Western US, Steinhart Aquarium and Morrison Planetarium return to Golden Gate Park in late 2008, their new home

An antique cable car on display at the Cable Car Barn Museum

will have an undulating grassy roof, a partially enclosed plaza, and a modernistic design by architect Renzo Piano. Until then, a temporary downtown facility close to other SOMA museums keeps the focus alive, with fish and reptiles in tanks, swimming penguins, and changing exhibits ranging from leaf-cutter ants to climate change in Californian bio-regions. Scientists in the field contribute to information on display, with constant updates on new species identification and documentation of animal behaviour, including online dispatches from a research site in Madagascar.

The California Academy of Sciences is typical of the American passion for creating museums that can educate adults and children in an unstupefying way. Up close is the way to see natural wonders, and there's barely a glass window or barrier between animals, swimmers, crawlers and the wonderful collections that have been painstakingly brought back from around the world since 1853.

Location until late 2008: 875 Howard Street, SOMA. Tel: (415) 321 8000; www.calacademy.org.
Open: daily 10am–5pm. Admission charge (free first Wed of the month).
Metro: Powell.

California Palace of the Legion of Honor

California Palace of the Legion of Honor

Prestigiously located in the northwest corner of Lincoln Park, this fine arts museum was built in 1924 by the sugar baron Adolph Spreckels and his wife Alma. It is dedicated to the Californians who fell on French battlefields in World War I, and was designed in Beaux-Arts style by George Applegarth as a replica of the Hôtel de Salm in Paris. It was there that Napoleon Bonaparte established the Légion d'Honneur, the premier military and civil order of merit in France.

Renovation included the addition of a sky-lit courtyard surrounded by six lower-level galleries where special exhibitions are held. There is also a theatre, bookstore, restaurant and a café with views out to the Pacific Ocean.

The museum's permanent collection spans 4,000 years of ancient and European art from 2500 BC to this century. There are major masterpieces by artists such as El Greco, Rembrandt, Watteau, Monet and Picasso. Exhibits range from tapestries, costumes and porcelain to a rich array of books, prints and drawings collected by the Achenbach Foundation for Graphic Arts. A key attraction is a collection of over 70 sculptures by Rodin – one of the several casts made of his famous bronze *Le Penseur* greets visitors arriving in the Palace's colonnaded front courtyard.
Lincoln Park, 34th Ave and Clement St. Tel: (415) 863 3330; www.thinker.org Open: Tue–Sun 9.30am–5pm. Admission charge (free, first Tue of the month). Bus: 1, 2, 18, 38.

The Cannery at Delmonte Square

The least gaudy of the shopping and entertainment complexes lining Fisherman's Wharf, the red-brick Cannery was built in 1907 and was once the largest peach canning factory in the world. Today its warehouses and tree-lined courtyards are used to pack in tourists with the help of street performers, souvenir shops, clothes boutiques, art galleries, a jazz club, and a please-everyone range of restaurants and cafés.
2801 Leavenworth St at Beach St. Tel: (415) 771 3112; www.delmontesquare.com Free admission. Cable car: Powell/Hyde. Bus: 30 & 47. MUNI: F-Line.

Museum of the City of San Francisco

An absorbing miscellany of San Franciscan memorabilia makes this small museum worth seeking out. Some of its exhibits are commendably bizarre and monumental, such as the golden head from the 6.7-m (22-ft) high illuminated statue of the Goddess of Progress that capped City Hall prior to the 1906 earthquake, and an oversized, hideous, laughing Sal figure, raucously cackling at the entrance.

Other finds reflect the human details of city life – crockery fused together by the heat of the 1906 post-earthquake conflagration, atmospheric old photographs of Chinatown, and a commemorative souvenir bearing the lyrics of 'I Left my Heart in San Francisco'.

Temporary exhibits are at Pier 45 (Fisherman's Wharf). The museum moves to the Old San Francisco mint in future years. www.sfhistory.org. MUNI: F-line.

Inside the Museum of the City of San Francisco near Fisherman's Wharf

The Cannery: one of the best of San Francisco's many shopping and dining complexes

Visitors enjoying the sunshine outside the Yerba Buena Center for the Arts

Cartoon Art Museum

Constantly popping up in newspapers, magazines, adverts and animated films, cartoon art is a brash and colourful squatter in the palace of American culture. This museum has a permanent collection of around 6,000 examples dating from the 1730s, and mounts seven annual exhibitions. Close to Yerba Buena Gardens, its facilities include a cartoon classroom and bookstore.
655 Mission St. Tel: (415) 227 8666; www.cartoonart.org Open: Tue–Sun 11am–5pm. Admission charge ('pay what you wish' first Tue of every month). Metro: Powell. Bus: 12, 14, 30.

Castro

Whatever your sexuality, San Francisco's world-famous gay neighbourhood is worth seeing (*see pp42–3*). Contrary to the reservations of many tourists, it is safe for both men and women and a fun place to shop, drink and spend time. While there are a few seedy bars, as there are in all parts of the city, the neighbourhood is a flourishing tribute to the 'pink economy' and the warmth and humour of its residents.

The best introduction to the history and achievements of the Castro is to take a guided walking tour (*see p29*). Two blocks in Castro Street, from Market Street south to 19th Street, form its core, and are signposted by the 1922 Castro Theatre – a classic old-style movie palace complete with ascending Wurlitzer organ. Though its shops and bars come and go, several have become neighbourhood landmarks, such as Cliff's Variety hardware store, a heaven for homebuilders and frock makers, and the gay and lesbian bookstore, A Different Light. On the eastern corner with Market Street, the Twin Peaks Bar pioneered the coming out of the Castro by having large picture windows and an openly gay clientele for all the world to admire.

Wax Museum at Fisherman's Wharf

It's hard to predict just whom you'll spot at San Francisco's only wax museum. This San Francisco institution has its own collection of Gold Rush miners and local heroes such as footballers Steve Young and Joe Montana who led the 49ers to Super Bowl fame more times than opposing teams like to count.

The four-floor museum is a maze of walkways designed to startle visitors with surprise sightings of celebrities from the past few thousand years of human history. Along with modern faces such as US President George W Bush and Britain's Queen Elizabeth II, the wax museum features the likes of comedian and actor Robin Williams, singer Britney Spears and Latin idol Ricky Martin. Political leaders tend to stay on view for years, but cultural icons come and go. But not every celeb gets waxed. With space for about 300 figures, the Wax Museum asks visitors who they would most like to see reproduced. Only the most frequently requested personalities get the full treatment. Recent additions include Eminem, Angelina Jolie, Denzel Washington and Jackie Chan.
145 Jefferson St, Fisherman's Wharf.
Tel: (800) 439 4305;
www.waxmuseum.com Open: Mon–Fri 10am–9pm, Sat & Sun 9am–11pm.

Admission charge. MUNI:
F-Line, Cable Car: Powell/Hyde,
Powell/Mason.

Yerba Buena Center for the Arts
Opened in 1993 as part of the Yerba Buena Gardens development (*see p97*), this multi-million dollar arts centre combines art galleries, film and performance theatres, a gift shop and the OPTS Café. A major venue for travelling exhibitions and performers, its cultural agenda reflects a commitment to promoting Bay Area artists and the diversity of its communities.
701 Mission St at Third St.
Tel: (415) 978 2787;
www.ybca.org/b-ybca.html
Galleries open: Tue–Sun 11am–5pm (till 8pm first Thur of the month).
Closed: Mon. Admission charge (free first Tue of every month).
Metro: Montgomery, Powell. Bus: 5, 9, 14, 15, 30, 38, 45.

Yerba Buena Center for the Arts with the San Francisco Museum of Modern Art behind

San Francisco's gay and lesbian community came to the fore in the 1970s and is now firmly established in the mainstream of its life. The city's reputation as a gay haven emerged during World War II, when the US military systematically expelled homosexuals from their ranks – for those serving in the Pacific arena, that meant the port of San Francisco. Rather than go home to hostility, the servicemen formed their own enclaves here.

A second gay immigration followed during the McCarthy era, when homosexuals were purged from government positions. In the 1960s antagonism by the police and the wooing of the gay vote by liberal politicians brought gay rights issues into the open. As the hippy revolution endorsed more liberated lifestyles, San Franciscan gays drifted from Haight-Ashbury into the cheap housing of the nearby Castro District.

Today the Castro is the archetypal gay neighbourhood (see p40), though what might have been a fairy-tale evolution from ghetto to mecca has been marred by two tragedies that have ultimately proved catalytic rallying points. The first was the murder of the openly homosexual politician Harvey Milk, who was elected a city Supervisor in 1977. He was gunned down on 27 November 1978 by Dan White, a disaffected former policeman who became infuriated by Milk's liberal policies. White's trial provoked angry demonstrations, and now Harvey Milk has joined the pantheon of martyred American political heroes.

In 1981 AIDS surfaced, cooling the party atmosphere in the Castro and causing devastating losses by the mid-1980s. San Francisco's gays and lesbians have been at the

forefront of the response to this worldwide epidemic.

Gay and lesbian life in San Francisco is no longer confined to the Castro – Valencia Street in the Mission, for example, has several lesbian and feminist stores and meeting places. Conversely, celebrations such as Halloween and Pride Weekend (late June) with a parade down Market Street, now attract many straight San Franciscans to the Castro.

Facing page above: Castro stars; below: gay couple dressed for a street celebration
Above: gay seniors riding motorised cable car in the San Francisco Pride Parade; right: float in San Francisco Pride Parade, downtown San Francisco

Chinatown

Most of the Chinese who have traditionally settled in America trace their roots back to Guangdong province, an area on the coast of southeast China of similar size to the Bay Area. Many came initially as unskilled labour, working in the gold rush mines tailings, as farmworkers, and providing 90 per cent of the workforce that constructed the Central Pacific Railroad. San Francisco was their port of arrival, and it was here that they established their largest enclave. By 1880 Chinatown had 21,000 inhabitants, though only a thousand of these were women.

Always busy, the streets of Chinatown are lined with brightly coloured lights and signs

The fires ignited by the 1906 earthquake not only destroyed the old Chinatown but its immigration records too, enabling many Chinese to claim American citizenship and bring their children across the Pacific. The community backed the 1911 revolution against the Manchu dynasty and the Nationalist cause in the long-running feud with mainland Communist China. Today San Francisco's Chinese-American community is spread far beyond Chinatown – a second enclave has emerged around Clement Street in the Richmond District, a third in the Sunset District. Oakland has yet another Chinatown.

Grant Avenue

The entrance gate to Chinatown is at the south end of Grant Avenue at Bush Street. Grant Avenue is the neighbourhood's high street, packed with shops and restaurants with bright façades that attract both tourists and residents. (*Also see pp46–7.*)

Bank of Canton

Nothing brings home the complexity of Chinatown better than the story of the Chinatown Telephone Exchange. This vivid, pagoda-roofed building, which now belongs to the Bank of Canton, was constructed in 1909 and was the first post-earthquake building to be demonstratively Chinese in appearance.

DIM-SUM

There is no better introduction to the immense variety of flavours and textures in Cantonese food than a *dim-sum* meal. Served from mid-morning to mid-afternoon, this is a refreshingly menu-free experience. Diners choose from a passing trolley laden with sweet and savoury Chinese delicacies – dumplings stuffed with meat and fish, spring rolls, deep-fried dishes, steamed buns and the elaborate specialities of the house. Bills are calculated by the number of saucers you pile up.

Designed like a temple, it housed a unique foreign-language telephone exchange that required operators not only to speak English and five Chinese dialects but also memorise 2,100 residents' names and their phone numbers. When a long-distance call came in, a runner would be sent dashing down the alleys – a pool of male and female messengers was kept on stand-by and fired off according to the sex of the recipient. The Exchange closed in 1949 when the duller world of automation arrived.
743 Washington St.

Chinese Culture Center of San Francisco

This small exhibition space and shop in the Hilton San Francisco Financial District Hotel puts on changing shows relevant to the Chinese-American heritage. It also arranges historical and culinary tours of Chinatown.
750 Kearny St, Third Floor. Tel: (415) 986 1822; www.c-c-c.org. Open: Tue–Sat 10am–4pm. Free admission.

Chinese Historical Society of America

This museum is a highly informative crash course in the history of the Chinese community in San Francisco and America. It is a gripping story that starts in the exploited days of the coolie trade, moves to the racist hostility and exclusionary immigration laws of the 1880s, rides out the 1906 earthquake, then progresses through the 'gilded ghetto' days of postwar Chinatown to the open society of today.
*965 Clay St. Tel: (415) 391 1188;
www.chsa.org
Open: Tue–Fri noon–5pm, Sat–Sun noon–4pm.
Closed: Mon. Admission charge
(free first Thur of the month).*

Old St Mary's Church
See p46.

Portsmouth Square
*See pp86–7.
Cable car: California St.
Bus: 1, 15, 30, 45.*

Buildings along Grant Avenue in Chinatown

Walk: Chinatown

San Francisco's best-known neighbourhood is safe, compact and packed with life and colour. This introductory walk around its main sights reveals the history in its hectic streets. The ideal time is on a Tue–Sun afternoon, when the Chinese Historical Society is open. *See also pp44–5.*

Allow 1½ hours.

The walk starts at the southern entrance to Chinatown at the junction of Grant Ave and Bush St.

1 Chinatown Gate

The Chinatown Gate, roofed with green tiles and animated dragons, welcomes visitors to the neighbourhood's principal street, Grant Avenue. Built in 1970, the gate is part of a continuing effort to enhance the commercial image and tourist appeal of Chinatown.

Walk up Grant Ave to the corner of Pine St. Turn right and cross the street into St Mary's Square, next to Quincy St. Walking through you pass a steel-cloaked statue of the revolutionary Nationalist leader Dr Sun Yat-Sen, who lived in Chinatown prior to the overthrow of the Manchu dynasty in 1911.

2 Old St Mary's Church

On the corner of Grant Avenue and California Street rises the red-brick Roman Catholic church of Old St Mary's. Dedicated in 1854, California's first cathedral's early congregations were predominantly Irish. A solemn warning on the clocktower – 'Son, Observe the Time and Fly from Evil' – still advises visitors to flee the brothels and opium dens that once made Chinatown notorious.

Turn right into Grant Ave. At the next junction turn left up Sacramento St, then right into Waverly Place.

3 Waverly Place

One of the most delightful streets in Chinatown, Waverly Place begins with

the First Chinese Baptist Church. Its dark, rubble-faced walls were constructed with bricks salvaged from the debris of the 1906 earthquake. Many of the buildings here were built with elaborately painted balconies by Chinese benevolent associations and incorporate temples in their upper floors.
Cross Clay St. At the end of Waverly Place turn left into Washington St, then immediately right into Ross Alley.

4 Ross Alley
Typical of the narrow alleys hidden within Chinatown, Ross Alley is a reminder of the backstreet sweatshops where many Chinese women work. A sweet biscuit smell wafts from the Golden Gate Fortune Cookie Company at No. 56 – despite its traditional association with Chinese cuisine, the cookie with an inner motto was actually invented in 1909 by the Japanese manager of the Tea Garden in Golden Gate Park.
Turn right down Jackson St to reach Grant Ave. Turn right and walk one block, turning left into Washington St. Note the ornate Bank of Canton at No. 743, formerly the Chinatown Telephone Exchange (see pp44–5). Continue into Portsmouth Square.

5 Portsmouth Square
This historic square is now the social focus of Chinatown (*see pp86–7*).
Cross the square to reach Kearny St. Turn right on to Clay St for three blocks.

6 Chinese Historical Society of America
At 965 Clay Street, this small but highly informative museum documents the

Chinese community's contribution to the story of San Francisco (*see p45*). You might also visit the Pacific Heritage Museum at 608 Commercial Street (*see p82*).
Retrace your steps back to Grant Ave. Turn right four blocks to return to the Chinatown Gate.

Built before the rise of Chinatown, Old St Mary's was San Francisco's first cathedral

Civic Center

The official heart, public smile and open arms (but not the soul) of San Francisco are contained within its Civic Center. Sitting in the triangle formed by the arteries of Van Ness Avenue and Market Street, this assembly of administrative offices, arts venues and public spaces reflects the civic zeal that erupted after the 1906 earthquake.
Metro: Civic Center. Bus: 5 & 21.

Asian Art Museum
The largest museum devoted to Asian art outside that continent is filled for the most part by the priceless collection of the late millionaire Avery Brundage, a long-serving president of the International Olympic Committee. Its 14,000 treasures cover 6,000 years of Asian art and include bronzes, porcelain, textiles, paintings, *netsuke* (Japanese miniatures) and Indian sculpture.

The museum's displays feature about 2,500 items at any one time arranged along three themes: the development of Buddhism across Asia; trade and cultural exchanges across Asia and beyond; and local beliefs and practices. Geographic highlights include India, the Persian world and West Asia (Afghanistan, Iran, Iraq, Turkmenistan, Uzbekistan), Southeast Asia, the Himalayas and Tibetan Buddhism, China, Korea and Japan. Treasures include the oldest known dated Chinese Buddha, from AD 338; the only gallery in the western hemisphere devoted to Sikh art; 2,000 years of Indian religious objects reflecting Hindu, Buddhist, Muslim, Sikh and Jain traditions; an encyclopaedic collection of Chinese pottery from every time period and every major kiln in the country; and the most complete collection of Korean art outside Korea. A special exhibitions programme focuses on contemporary art from Asia.

In 2003, the Asian moved from Golden Gate Park to what was once the San Francisco Main Library in the Civic Center. The 1917 Beaux-Arts style library building was transformed by architect Gae Aulenti.
200 Larkin St. Tel: (415) 581 3500; www.asianart.org Open: Tue–Sun 10am–5pm (till 9pm on Thur). Admission charge (free first Tue of every month).

Civic Center Plaza looking out from Asian Art Museum to the dome of the City Hall

City Hall
Designed by Arthur Brown Jr and John Bakewell Jr in 1915, City Hall epitomises the vogue for the Beaux-Arts style rampant at that time. Both architects had been students of the influential École des Beaux-Arts in Paris, which sang the virtues of the colossal, the symmetrical and the classical. Its baroque dome is modelled on St Peter's

in Rome, and the parade of allegorical sculpture on the pediment above the Polk Street entrance is by the French artist Henri Crenier. Its figures depict high-minded notions like the Wealth of California, Trade and Navigation. Round the back, the relentless traffic on Van Ness Avenue appears to have little time for Wisdom, Learning and Truth.
Dr Carlton & Goodlett Place. For tours tel: (415) 554 4933; www.sfgov.org Open: Mon–Fri 8am–8pm.

Civic Center Plaza

This tree-lined plaza in front of City Hall sometimes becomes an animated protest arena, but for much of the year it serves as an open-air dormitory for the homeless. Begging can be a problem at times, so visitors should exercise caution. Underneath the plaza is Brooks Hall, a conference centre, and on the south side the 1915 Bill Graham Civic Auditorium, named in honour of the rock music impresario. On the north side is the 1922 Old State Building.

West of Van Ness Avenue

Built parallel with City Hall are the War Memorial Opera House and the Veterans' Building, both completed in 1932 and dedicated to the soldiers of World War I. To their north is the 1986 New State Building, prominently

displaying the Seal of California. South of the opera house is the 1980 Louise M Davies Symphony Hall.

San Francisco Main Library

Built in 1996, this brilliant white building designed by architect IM Pei replaced the original 1917 library building damaged in the 1989 Loma Prieta earthquake. The redesigned old library building at Larkin and McAllister streets is now the Asian Art Museum.
100 Larkin St at Grove St. Tel: (415) 557 4400; http://sfpl.lib.ca.us Library open: Tue–Thur 9am–8pm, Fri noon–6pm, Sat 10am–6pm, Sun noon–5pm, Mon 10am–6pm. Free admission.

United Nations Plaza

East of Hyde Street stands the Federal Building, and beside it the United Nations Plaza with an equestrian statue of Simón Bolivar, the liberator of South America. The plaza commemorates the signing of the UN Charter in 1945 in the nearby War Memorial Opera House. The Heart of the City Farmers' Market takes place here every Wednesday and Sunday.
Market, Hyde, and McAllister Sts.

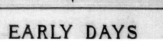

EARLY DAYS

Christianity comes to the Indian – imperious figures on the Lick Monument, Civic Center

Cliff House

Perched on the headlands of Point Lobos, with the windswept runway of Ocean Beach stretching southward, the Cliff House is where San Francisco conducts its long-running romance with the seaside. The leading protagonist is Adolph Sutro, a philanthropic German immigrant who made a fortune from building a drainage tunnel for the Comstock silver mines in the 1870s and then became a property developer and San Francisco mayor. He and his family lived just across the Great Highway in what is now Sutro Heights Park (*see p131*).

The present Cliff House, dating from 1909, is but a faint shadow of the grand,

The seaside palace built by Adolf Sutro in 1896

eight-storey mock-château that Sutro built on the site in 1896. This ornate Victorian palace, with its dining rooms, dance floors and observation tower, formed the flamboyant centrepiece in a bathing resort that included the Sutro Baths and a railway line to bring daytrippers from the city. That building burned down in 1907, but is well remembered in the many photographs displayed around today's Cliff House. The Cliff House is part of the Golden Gate National Recreation Area. The main building has been restored back to the 1909 design. Inside the Cliff House is Sutro's Restaurant, Sutro's Bar, casual Bistro, and a gift shop.
*Tel: (415) 561 4323;
www.nps.gov/goga/clho*

Point Lobos

The Spanish named this part of the coast after the barking *lobos marinos* (sea wolves) they found living among its rocks and waters. Sea lions still cavort around the guano-coated Seal Rocks off the Cliff House, where you can also see a variety of seabirds, including black cormorants, brown pelicans and gulls.

Ruins of the Sutro Baths, once furnished with stained glass and classical sculptures

Sutro Baths

Covering 1.2 hectares (3 acres) north of the Cliff House, the ruins of the world's largest bathhouse make a poignant sight among the rocks. Opened in 1896, the Sutro Baths once accommodated 24,000 swimmers in seven variable-temperature saltwater and freshwater pools. The number of visitors gradually dwindled after World War I and the baths were turned into an ice rink, then burned down in 1966.

Cliff House is located at 1066–1090 Point Lobos Ave. Bus: 38 & 38L.

Coit Tower

See p92.

Embarcadero

Curving round the city's northeastern corner from China Basin to Fisherman's Wharf, this 10-km (6-mile) waterfront illustrates San Francisco's gradual transition from thriving port to international leisure centre. At its centre stands the landmark Ferry Building, commandingly sited at the end of Market Street. Built in 1898, its clock tower was modelled on the Giralda in Seville. It still functions as a ferry terminus, reminiscent of the great city gateway through which 50 million passengers once poured annually – a stream stemmed by the opening of the Bay and Golden Gate Bridges. Renovated and re-opened with shops, food stalls and restaurants in 2003, the Ferry Building is once again lively.

The Ferry Plaza Farmers' Market is a Saturday and Tuesday year-round attraction (also open spring–autumn, Thur and Sun), with food, flowers, preserves, meat, fish and chef cooking demonstrations. *Tel: (415) 291 3276.*

North of the Ferry Building, the Embarcadero's piers bear odd numbers. Pier 7 has been converted into a restful waterside promenade, others now house offices and studios, and cruise liners dock at Pier 35. To the south, beyond the Bay Bridge, the piers have even numbers. Known as South Beach, this area is now gentrifying with new apartments, restaurants, a palm tree-lined promenade, and a baseball venue, AT & T Park.

Cliff House, near Point Lobos

Exploratorium

Imagine a mad scientist's workshop invaded by a school trip, and you have the rough-and-ready, hands-on, kid-friendly, back-of-the-garage world of the Exploratorium. Running behind the Palace of Fine Arts (*see p82*), with plans to move to the waterfront in the future, this hangar-like laboratory rejoices in the mysteries of natural phenomena, and then sets you working it all out with all necessary tools provided. If it's raining and the kids are looking glum, this is your salvation.

The Transamerica Pyramid – a beacon amid the skyscrapers of the Financial District

Built on two floors, the Exploratorium is loosely divided into areas exploring subjects like Resonance, Weather and Electricity, with plenty of exhorting commands like 'Create a Mini-Tornado!' and 'Sing into Vidium!' beside the exhibits. The result is baffling and enjoyable entertainment for both children and adults, backed up by a gift store and very necessary café. Many of the most fascinating interactions are designed by artists-in-residence, like the pop video-style *Recollections* by Ed Tannebaum. The most popular exhibit is the Tactile Dome, a completely dark crawl-round geodesic dome which you explore through touch, and which requires prior reservation.
3601 Lyon St at Marina Blvd. Tel: (415) 397 5673; www.exploratorium.edu Tactile Dome reservations tel: (415) 561 0362 (over-seven only). Open: Tue–Sun 10am–5pm. Closed Mon. Admission charge (free first Wed of the month). Bus: 28, 29, 30, 43.

Financial District

Strolling between skyscrapers is one of the particular joys of America's great cities, and San Francisco's compact but extremely elevated Financial District presents a classic mix of historic and contemporary big money architecture (*see pp98–9*).

The city's tallest building is the 260-m (853-ft) Transamerica Pyramid (*see p93*), closely followed by the 237-m (778-ft) carnelian-clad 555 California Street, formerly known as the Bank of America Building, and the 212-m (695-ft) First Interstate Center (345 California Street), where the top 11 floors are occupied by the luxury Mandarin Oriental Hotel. Much of the eastern corner of the Financial District is given over to the eight-block Embarcadero Center, which combines shops, restaurants, offices and the Hyatt Regency San Francisco. The latter hotel is crowned by the revolving Equinox restaurant where you can enjoy a leisurely overview of these pillars of money.
In the triangle formed by Kearny, Market and Washington sts. Cable car: California St. Metro: Montgomery, Embarcadero. Bus: 1 & 15.

Fisherman's Wharf

Fisherman's Wharf may be the city's most visited attraction, which is a pity, as it has little to do with the real and memorable San Francisco. Its frenzied parade of low-rise hotels, shopping centres, souvenir shops, seafood stalls and waterfront restaurants runs east from Aquatic Park to the climactic consumerism of Pier 39 (*see p83*). Providing you forestall disappointment by going in the full knowledge that it is shamelessly devoted to tourist-wooing commerce, you will emerge poorer but mentally unscathed.

In the 1860s there was just a beach here (now Beach Street), but by the start of the 20th century so many Genoese and Sicilian boats were moored here the area was known as 'Italy Harbor'. Its days as a hard-working wharf are all but over, but an air of salty realism lingers down unfragrant walkways like Fish Alley and Pier 47, and beside Jefferson Lagoon where the sports fishing boats tie up. Ferries to Alcatraz and Sausalito leave from Pier 41. (*See also relevant entries for* Hyde Street Pier (*see p70*), *the* Cannery *at Del Monte Square* (*see p38*), USS *Pampanito* (*see p96*), *and* SS *Jeremiah O'Brien.*)

Jefferson St. www.fishermanswharf.org
Cable car: Powell/Hyde, Powell/Mason.
MUNI: F-Line.

SS *Jeremiah O'Brien*

This is the last unaltered example of the 2,700 Liberty ships built at great speed to carry cargo in World War II. The spartan SS *Jeremiah O'Brien* was constructed in Maine in 1943 in just 57 days and made several transatlantic crossings in the run-up to D-Day. A 1994 commemorative trip to join the 50th anniversary celebrations of the Allied invasion proved that the ship remains fighting fit.

Pier 45, Fisherman's Wharf. Tel: (415) 544 0100; www.ssjeremiahobrien.org
Open: daily 10am–4pm.
Occasional cruises for additional charge.
Admission charge.

Ferry trips, Bay cruises and Alcatraz tours depart from Fisherman's Wharf: here, Pier 39

Cable-car ride: Fisherman's Wharf

Cable cars have been carrying locals and visitors around the city since 1873, and are a quintessential feature of San Francisco. This tour (*see map on pp30–31*) rides the famous lines linking Downtown and Fisherman's Wharf. Early in the morning or at sunset are the most magical times for this ride.

Allow 1½ hours excluding time spent queuing.

The Powell & Hyde Street cable car up Hyde Street from Fisherman's Wharf

The ride starts next to Hallidie Plaza, at the junction of Powell and Market sts.

1 Hallidie Plaza
Named after the inventor of San Francisco's cable car system (*see p24*), the focus near the plaza is a manually operated turnaround for the cars. In high season long queues are inevitable, for no visitors leave unless they have ridden a cable car. This tour starts with the more popular Powell/Hyde line (marked 'Beach & Hyde' on the front), but you will not miss anything if you follow the itinerary in reverse and take a Powell/Mason car (marked 'Bay & Taylor' on the front).

2 Powell/Hyde Line
Try to sit or stand by the open-air seats on the right-hand side. The car trundles north past Union Square, then climbs Nob Hill to halt by the back of the Fairmont Hotel and the crossover with the California Street line. The descent down Powell Street offers views north across the Bay to Angel Island and east to the towers of the Financial District.

After swinging left along Jackson Street, the car turns into Hyde Street. The undulating streets ahead seem perfect for a classic San Francisco car chase. Distant to the left are the woods of the Presidio, to the right Lombard Street, part of which is the famous 'Crookedest Street' (*see pp72–3*). From here it is an exhilarating descent to the Bay – ahead you can see the tall ships of Hyde Street Pier, with Alcatraz beyond.
Disembark at the final stop and walk down Hyde St towards the Bay.

3 Fisherman's Wharf

Fisherman's Wharf is packed with restaurants, shops and attractions and can seem oppressively commercial when very busy. One antidote is to pause for a spell in Aquatic Park (*see p36*) to the left, or inspect the evocative historic ships of Hyde Street Pier (*see p70*) ahead. Turn right into Jefferson Street for the main parade. On the right you pass two shopping complexes, The Cannery (*see p38*) and, by Leavenworth Street, Anchorage Square. Continue past the bubbling seafood stalls, souvenir shops and fishing boats to reach the centre of Fisherman's Wharf – heralded by a sign resembling a ship's wheel.
Turn right into Taylor St. Three blocks south, at the junction with Bay St, is the Powell/Mason cable-car terminus.

4 Powell/Mason Line

Try to sit on the left of the car. The return ride begins with a swing left down Columbus Avenue, offering glimpses of Washington Square, Coit Tower and the Transamerica Pyramid. The car then turns into Mason Street,

Start spending now!

climbing up Russian Hill. Passing the Cable Car Barn and Museum from which the entire system is controlled (*see p36–7*), the ride swings into Powell Street and travels along the western side of Chinatown.

After climbing up to the California Street junction, the car pulls back towards Market Street, providing fine views across the south of the city centre.
The ride concludes by Hallidie Plaza.

'Everybody was gracious. The most perfect courtesy obtained. Never, in all San Francisco's history, were her people so kind and courteous as on this night of terror.' Thus Jack London described the aftermath of the earthquake of 18 April 1906, the worst in American history.

Estimated at 8.3 on the Richter Scale, the 1906 'quake lasted for less than a minute but devastated much of the city. Hampered by burst water mains and collapsed buildings, fire crews were unable to contain the ensuing blazes that ravaged the city for three days. Some 3,000–6,000 citizens are thought to have died, and a great stretch of the city's northeast corner was reduced to rubble.

Within six years San Francisco had been rebuilt, but the memory of this cataclysm lingers in its psyche. Every resident knows it could happen again, any time, and few visitors leave without wondering if it's living on the fault line that puts the zing in this audacious city.

On 17 October 1989 it did happen again – scoring 7.1 this time and causing over 60 deaths in the Bay Area. Known as 'Loma Prieta' from its epicentre near Santa Cruz, the earthquake brought down a section of the Bay Bridge and buildings in the Marina, and provoked the demolition of the waterfront Embarcadero freeway – now considered a blessing.

San Franciscans remain phlegmatic about this ever-imminent catastrophe. Loma Prieta inspired black-humoured souvenirs like wobbly mugs and Richter Scale Ale.

Buildings close for 'seismic retro-fit', office-workers conduct earthquake drills, shops advise worried tourists to hide under the table – but all San Franciscans know that the only worthwhile safety measure is to get as much happiness and partying under your belt while you can. They understand that the planet is a-rippling and a-rumbling all the time, so don't be surprised if you're driving down the freeway and the soft-spoken DJ on the radio prefaces the next track with a nonchalant announcement that 'Mother Earth has just had another of her little tremors'.

Facing page: City Hall was damaged in the 1989 earthquake and took four years to renovate
Right: around 14,000 Victorian homes remain in San Francisco, despite the fact that 514 blocks burned down following the 1906 earthquake
Below: Loma Prieta brought down a section of the Bay Bridge

Fort Mason Center

Occupying a prime location on the city's northernmost promontory, the buildings and grounds of Fort Mason exemplify the San Franciscans' laudable knack for turning former military posts into bases for cultural activity. Originally fortified by the Spanish in 1797, the site was taken over by squatters in the gold rush and then made into a US Army post during the Civil War. Its busiest hour came in World War II, when 1.5 million troops passed through en route to the Pacific war zones. In 1962 its military duties transferred to Oakland, and it has, since 1977, been included as part of the Golden Gate National Recreation Area.

Masks are among many colourful goods on sale at the Mexican Museum gift shop

The Fort Mason Center now inhabits the waterside piers and wooden warehouses, while other historic buildings are used by the GGNRA and resource conservation organisations. There are museums and theatres, special events, and the acclaimed vegetarian restaurant Greens (*see p164*), which looks on to the Bay, that make a trip here worthwhile.
www.fortmason.org

Museo Italo-Americano
The museum works towards preservng the heritage of Italian-Americans by staging exhibitions of Italian art and culture and work by Italian-American artists.
Building C. Tel: (415) 673 2200;
www.museoitaloamericano.org
Open: Wed–Sun noon–4pm.
Admission charge (free first Wed of every month).

Mexican Museum
Dedicated to Mexican and Mexican-American culture, this museum presents exhibitions around San Francisco drawn from its own permanent collection and from the art of Latin America. Its gift store, La Tienda, has a notable selection of Mexican textiles, tin mirrors, masks and other aesthetic crafts. The museum plans to reopen its galleries when it moves to a new location in Yerba Buena Gardens Arts District.
Building D. Tel: (415) 202 9700;
www.mexicanmuseum.org
Open: Wed–Sat 11am–5pm.

The main entrance of Fort Mason Center is at Marina Blvd by Buchanan St. Tel: (415) 345 7544, (415) 345 3400; www.fortmason.org. Bus: 10, 22, 28, 30, 47, 49, 82X. Walkers can also follow Golden Gate Promenade west from Aquatic Park.

Fort Point National Historic Site

Tucked under the carcass of Golden Gate Bridge, Fort Point was constructed between 1853 and 1861 to defend the city and Bay, but has never fired a shot in anger. It must have been a bleak posting, judging by the memoirs of one lighthouse keeper who recorded in 1915 that 'there is the ocean and the sand and the guns and the soldiers. That is all. It grows monotonous.'

Fort Point is still as chilly as ever, but there is a satisfaction in its functional military architecture, weathered brickwork, and the arsenal of historic cannon and guns displayed within its massive walls. Amongst these is a bronze cannon of 1684 that has miraculously survived from the original late 18th-century Spanish settlement. A museum displays military uniforms, equipment, photographs and menus suggesting that the early 19th-century US soldier ate an

World War II

The Japanese attack on Hawaii on 7 December 1941 had a long-lasting effect on San Francisco. The port became the chief embarkation point for the war in the Pacific, its coastal headlands were fortified against invasion, and naval shipbuilding yards were constructed at Sausalito and Richmond. While Japanese-Americans were being arrested and interned, African-American civilians arrived to work in the docks and factories, settling in neighbourhoods such as Hunter's Point and the Western Addition. At the end of the war in 1945 many soldiers and workers stayed on, transforming the social matrix of the city forever.

Once occupied by the military, the buildings of Fort Mason are now used for cultural activities

The shops of Ghirardelli Square are a must for souvenir hunters and chocolate lovers

awful lot of meat hash and Irish stew. Other exhibits trace the contribution of women and African-Americans to military life and the four-year construction of the Golden Gate Bridge.

Fort Point is part of the Golden Gate National Recreation Area. Exhibitions of cannon firing and drill in Civil War uniform are scheduled (call for times). *Tel: (415) 556 1693; www.nps.gov/fopo Open: Fri–Sun 10am–5pm. Closed: Mon–Thur until 2007 for Golden Gate Bridge retrofitting. Free admission. Bus: 28 & 29.*

Ghirardelli Square

Behind this much-publicised chocolate factory and shopping centre on the south side of Aquatic Park lies a classic San Franciscan tale of the gold rush immigrant made good. The Italian-born Domingo Ghirardelli arrived in the city in 1849 at the age of 32 to seek his fortune. Failing to strike it rich by prospecting, he resorted to the family trade of chocolate-making, setting up his first factory in 1852. In 1893 the business moved to the former woollen mills that have now become Ghirardelli Square. Today most of the company's confectionery is made elsewhere, but the historic machinery can be seen in sweet action in the Ghirardelli Chocolate Manufactory – a chocoholics' heaven that oozes with hot fudge, ice cream and sensual whirlpools of dark chocolate sauce.

Many of the other buildings on this red-brick manufacturing complex date from the start of the 20th century and originally produced cocoa, mustard and blankets. Among the shops and six eateries that now fill their levels, McCormick & Kuleto's Seafood Restaurant and the quality Mandarin (Chinese) Restaurant both enjoy fine views over the Bay.
900 North Point St at Larkin St. Tel: (415) 775 5500; www.ghirardellisq.com Cable car: Powell/Hyde. Bus: 19 & 30.

Golden Gate Bridge

Opened in 1937, the Golden Gate Bridge is one of the greatest in the world (*see pp106–7*). Many visitors assume its name derives from its shape and burning colour, but the strait between San Francisco and the Marin Headlands has been known as the Golden Gate since 1846. It was so christened by an exploring US Army officer, John C Frémont, in a respectful reference to the Golden Horn beside which Byzantium (now Istanbul) stood.

Used daily by an average 106,000 vehicles, the six-lane bridge has a line of tollbooths on its south side where drivers coming into the city must pay $5. There are vista points and parking at both ends facing the Bay side, and a main gift shop by Toll Plaza. You can walk or bicycle across, an epiphanic rite of passage that takes a good hour return – remember that it's cold and windy out there (*see p103*).

Highway 101. Tel: (415) 921 5858;
www.goldengate.org
Bus: 28 & also 76 on Sun only;
Golden Gate Transit.

A costumed interpreter explains the cannon firing at Fort Point

Golden Gate Park

A triumph of enlightened urban planning and visionary landscape gardening, the 412 hectares (1,017 acres) of Golden Gate Park stretch for over 5km (3 miles) from Stanyan Street west to Ocean Beach. Besides being a green lung with walks and gardens, the park has two popular city museums – the MH de Young Memorial Museum and the California Academy of Sciences that reopens in 2008. Cultural sights include a Japanese tea garden, windmills, historic statues and even a Buffalo Paddock. Leisure activities include boating, lawn bowling, tennis and golf, and a children's playground with a restored 1912 carousel (*see pp64–5*).

Japanese Tea Garden at the Golden Gate Park

Conservatory of Flowers
Inspired by London's Kew Gardens white glass, the conservatory was shipped over from Ireland in 1875 for the home of the millionaire James Lick. After his death it was erected in the park, and, refurbished in 2003, is now a resplendent Victorian greenhouse with lily-clad fish ponds, orchids, ferns and tropical trees.
In the northeast corner of the park by John F Kennedy Drive. Tel: (415) 666 7001; www.conservatoryofflowers.org Open: Tue–Sun 9am–4.30pm. Closed: Mon. Admission charge. Metro: N-line. Bus: 5, 7, 21, 33, 44 & 71.

Japanese Tea Garden
Built for the 1894 Midwinter International Exposition, these harmonious gardens are a dainty world of crooked paths, poetic bridges, meditative pools, blazing pagodas and a lush variety of plants and trees. A teahouse serves Japanese and Chinese teas, and it is easy to imagine visitors in top hats and parasols enjoying the gardens a century ago.
Hagiwara Tea Garden Drive. Tel: (415) 752 4227. Open: daily

Golden Gate Park

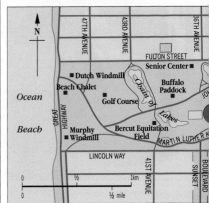

Purple iris and flowering bushes surround a lake at San Francisco Botanical Gardens at Strybing Arboretum

9am–6pm (call to check seasonal hours).
Admission charge. Bus: 44.

San Francisco Botanical Garden at Strybing Arboretum

Plants, trees and shrubs are laid out in geographical pockets from around the world, including a Garden of California Native Plants, redwood trees, and flora from South Africa, Australasia and Central America.
9th Ave at Lincoln Way. Tel: (415) 661 1316; www.sfbotanicalgarden.org
Open: Mon–Fri 8am–4.30pm,

weekends 10am–5pm.
Free admission. Metro: N-Line. Bus: 44.

Park tips
(Also check *www.parks.sfgov.org*)
- most points of interest are in the eastern half of the park
- on Sundays John F Kennedy Drive is closed to traffic between 19th Avenue and Stanyan Street
- free guided tours of the Japanese Tea Garden are offered by the San Francisco Parks Trust (*tel: (415) 750 5105; www.sfpt.org*)
- avoid the park at night

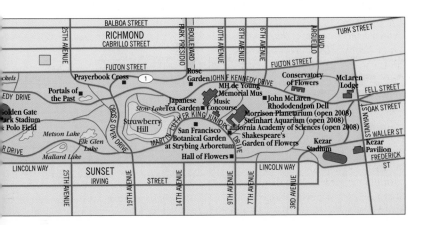

Walk: Golden Gate Park

Founded in 1870, Golden Gate Park is a country in the midst of a city. This walk introduces its most popular features (*see pp62–3*). Leave the park well before dark. *Allow from 1½ hours to half a day depending on how many museums and gardens you visit.*

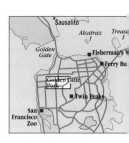

The walk starts at the northeast corner of Golden Gate Park at the junction of Fulton and Stanyan sts. Take Bus 21 from Market St.

1 To the Conservatory of Flowers

A path leads from the corner of Fulton and Stanyan streets into the park, curling down through the woods to Conservatory Drive. Cross this and continue straight on down the hill to a crossroads of four paths by a green bench. Turn right and keep on the path, which emerges by the dahlia beds on the east side of the Conservatory of Flowers (*see p62*).

2 To the MH de Young Memorial Museum

From the main entrance of the Conservatory of Flowers walk down the steps and bear right along a path to John F Kennedy Drive. Cross this road and turn right to walk along the adjacent path, marvelling at the relentless parade of joggers, skaters, roller-bladers, mountain bikers and even the odd walker. On the left you pass the John McLaren Rhododendron Dell with a statue of the devoted Scots park superintendent who shaped its landscape. This is followed by the upstanding figure of Chaplain William

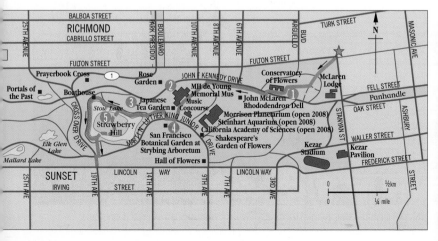

D McKinnon, then the Scots poet Robert Burns, and, turning left into Hagiwara Tea Garden Drive, the Reverend Thomas Starr-King. Continue past the statues of Junípero Serra and Miguel de Cervantes, passing a pair of sphinxes and the Cider Garden Press – all statues surviving from the 1894 California Midwinter Fair.

3 To the Japanese Tea Garden
The MH de Young Memorial Museum (*see p74*) stands to the right. Opposite, across the Music Concourse, will be the California Academy of Sciences re-opening in the park in 2008 (*see p37*). Continue along Hagiwara Tea Garden Drive. The shell-shaped bandstand, officially known as the Spreckels Temple of Music, dates from 1899. Beyond the de Young museum is the Japanese Tea Garden (*see p62*).

4 To the Botanical Garden at Strybing Arboretum
From the Japanese Tea Garden walk right to Martin Luther King Jr Drive. Cross the drive and enter San Francisco Botanical Garden at Strybing Arboretum (*see p63*).

5 Around Stow Lake
When you leave the Arboretum, cross the road again and take the path straight ahead. This runs round beside the Japanese Tea Garden. Turn left by the exit to walk up a hill and some steps. Turn right at the top, following a curving path that brings you to Stow Lake. Cross the road and bear right to walk beside the water. In the centre of the lake is the 130.5-m (428-ft) man-made Strawberry Hill, and a Chinese pagoda – a gift from the city of Taipei. The walk continues around the lake, past the boathouse where boats can be hired. A more energetic route is to cross the Roman bridge to climb Strawberry Hill for its views of the city, emerging by the rustic bridge on the south side. From this point walk downhill, past some toilets, to the jarringly busy junction of 19th Avenue and Lincoln Way.

Bus 71 from the opposite side of Lincoln Way goes back to Market St.

Stow Lake encircles the artificial island of Strawberry Hill and has boats for hire

Grace Cathedral

Set atop Nob Hill, this modern replica of the Notre-Dame cathedral in Paris was designed by Lewis P Hobart. Work began in 1927 but the building was not substantially finished until 1964. The doors of its main façade are copies of the famous Gates of Paradise designed by Ghiberti in 1424 for the Baptistery in Florence. Successful appeal has brought seismic reinforcements, a monumental staircase up to the main entrance, and an exterior courtyard labyrinth.

Despite its modernity, the church has a remarkable and enveloping spirituality. It is valued both as an official platform where respected leaders such as Martin Luther King Jr and Archbishop Desmond Tutu have preached, and as a force in the community – there are not many cathedrals in the world that have a basketball court underneath. An AIDS

Bronze door detail, Grace Cathedral

Interfaith Chapel has a striking altarpiece by sculptor Keith Haring.
1100 California St at Taylor St. Tel: (415) 749 6300; www.gracecathedral.org
Open: daily, but access restricted during services. Free admission.
Cable car: California. Bus: 1.

Haas-Lilienthal House

Exemplary of the Queen Anne style that dominated San Francisco's Victorian housing in the 1890s (*see pp84–5*), this imposing mansion is the headquarters of San Francisco Architectural Heritage, whose members provide guided tours. It was built in 1886 for a German-born immigrant, William Haas, who had a prosperous grocery business. The building was used as a family home by his heirs until 1972.

Graceful sculpture in Huntington Park, across from Grace Cathedral

While the house doesn't quite live up to Gelett Burgess's critical view that the ideal Queen Anne 'should be a restless, uncertain, frightful collection of details, giving the effect of a nightmare about to explode', it does bring home the haughty, cloistered lifestyle of the city's aspiring upper middle classes at that time. A basement museum provides books and information on the city's architectural heritage.

2007 Franklin St. Tel: (415) 441 3004; www.sfheritage.org/house.html
Open: Wed and Sat noon–3pm, Sun 11am–4pm. Admission charge.
Bus: 1, 12, 19, 27, 47, 49.

Haight-Ashbury

In the late 1960s San Francisco hosted one of the great spontaneous social experiments of the 20th century, the hippy revolution (*see pp68–9*). Its epicentre was Haight-Ashbury, a Victorian neighbourhood on the east side of Golden Gate Park that still clings to its counter-cultural roots and has the crazy street life to prove it. The best way to discover its haunts and history is to join a walking tour (*see pp28–9*); life gets wilder as the day goes on, so you may prefer to visit in the morning.

The core blocks of interest lie on Haight Street between Lyon and Stanyan streets. While some of the Victorian mansions have been so smartened up it's hard to imagine they were once squats and crash-pads for Hell's Angels and drug-high rock singers, there are still enough shops selling tie-dye clothes, chimes, Afghan imports and anarchist tracts to keep the joss-stick of hippy heritage burning. Notable landmarks include Magnolia Pub & Brewery (1398 Haight Street), once the infamous, marijuana-hazy Drogstore Café, the Haight-Ashbury Free Medical Clinic (558 Clayton Street), opened in 1967 and still dispensing free health care, and the hippy-revival Red Victorian Bed, Breakfast & Art (1665 Haight Street).

To the south lies the steep and wooded Buena Vista Park, to the north the green strip of the Panhandle, originally designed as a carriage entrance to Golden Gate Park. The area also has a second flowering, known as the Lower Haight, further east by the junction with Fillmore Street.
Bus: 6, 7, 33, 37, 43, 71.

The Haas-Lilienthal House and gardens

*I*f you're going to San Francisco', Scott McKenzie sang in 1967, 'be sure to wear some flowers in your hair.' In that year the Haight-Ashbury district became a psychedelic backdrop for the finest hours of the hippie movement, when the Bay Area's alternative clans massed for a 'Human Be-In' in Golden Gate Park and 500,000 flower children hit the city for the 'Summer of Love'.

'Hip' is thought to derive from Negro slang meaning 'to be informed'. The tuned-in and turned-on hippies shared the anti-establishment imperatives of their predecessors from North Beach, the Beat Generation, but took a more cosmic approach. Drugs, in particular LSD ('acid'), fuelled their search for a new awareness, which was supplemented by a passionate taste for long hair, Indian religion, second-hand velvet, wind chimes, tambourines, incense and – if you knew where to go – free love.

Though the legacy of this wave of Utopian anarchy has been enormous, it was but a brief, golden trip. By the autumn of 1967 violence and drug addiction were souring the dream, and 'Hashbury' (as it was quickly dubbed) became a magnet for unsavoury characters like the mass murderer Charles Manson. In October a 'Death of the Hippie' march was staged, and the tourist buses went elsewhere.

Today the Haight is gentrifying, and nostalgia for that hippie dawn thrives. Its greatest achievement was probably its music. Bands like Jefferson Airplane, Big Brother and the Holding Company (featuring Janis Joplin) and the long-playing Grateful Dead created the 'San Francisco Sound'. The magazine *Rolling Stone* was founded, and a new visual language appeared on record sleeves and Pop Art posters. If you missed the party, Tom Wolfe's *The Electric Kool-Aid Acid Test* gives a lively account of those heady days.

Hippy days when Haight-Ashbury was the centre of flower power and happy smoking

Hayes Valley

West of the Civic Center, the Hayes Valley is a resurgent neighbourhood born out of freeways brought down by the 1989 earthquake. Since then it has developed a reputation as a showcase for young and innovative designers, with an easy-going strip of interior design shops, art galleries, cafés and restaurants.
Hayes St by Laguna and Franklin sts. Bus: 21.

Hyde Street Pier

At the west end of Fisherman's Wharf, this is the best place to get a feel for San Francisco's maritime past. Moored up around the pier is a magnificent fleet of historic ships – some are still undergoing loving restoration – and there are also demonstrations of boatbuilding skills and a well-stocked

Frjtz restaurant and Gaia Tree Spa on Hayes Street

Maritime Store. The pier is the main attraction in the extensive San Francisco Maritime National Historical Park (*see p89*), and provides fine views of the city, Alcatraz and Golden Gate Bridge.
North end of Hyde St. Tel: (415) 447 5000; www.nps.gov/safr. Open: daily 9.30am–5pm (till 5.30pm in summer). Admission charge. Cable car: Powell/ Hyde. Metro: F-Line. Bus: 15.

CA Thayer

This three-masted schooner was built in 1895 to transport timber down the Pacific coast, and then later used to carry salted cod and salmon. There is a telling contrast between the captain's cosy, wood-panelled dining room and the grim forecastle bunks, where up to 28 crew slept on six-month cod fishing trips.

Eppleton Hall

This English-built paddle-wheel tug of 1914 is reminiscent of the vessels used in the Bay in gold rush times.

Craftsman at work on Hyde Street Pier

Balclutha

Built in Scotland in 1886, this stately square-rigged sailing ship carried cargo round the Cape Horn 17 times and visited ports throughout the world. Its towering masts and creaking decks are a romantic advert for the ocean life – providing you resided in the extraordinarily plush quarters reserved for the captain and his wife.

Alma

This flat-bottomed scow schooner was built in 1891 and is typical of the vessels once used for transporting bulky products such as hay and bricks across the Bay.

Eureka

Hyde Street Pier originally served as a car ferry terminal, and this steam-powered paddle-wheel ferryboat provides a nostalgic passage back to life in San Francisco before the bridging of the Bay. Built in 1890, she carried railway cars and then automobiles, and operated a regular service between this pier and Sausalito.

Barbary Coast

Prior to the 1906 earthquake, the area around Jackson Square became known as the 'Barbary Coast', a reference to the lawless Mediterranean coast of North Africa where Berber pirates once roamed. It was here that the abundantly male population of the gold rush days spent their wages, letting off steam in streets thick with bars, brothels, gambling houses and opium dens. The verb 'shanghai', where men were drugged and kidnapped to serve as hands on ships bound for the Far East, originates from this time. (For details on the 6-km (3¹/₂-mile) Barbary Coast Trail route check the interactive map on *www.sfhistory.org*)

Hercules

This 1907 tugboat originally burned oil, towing barges and sailing ships, including the nearby *CA Thayer*, around San Francisco, and north to Washington State.

Jackson Square Historic District

On the northern fringes of the Financial District, this protected area of predominantly 19th-century commercial buildings escaped the devastation caused by the 1906 earthquake. Its heart lies close to the Transamerica Pyramid, in Jackson Street between Montgomery and Sansome Streets, and is now occupied by antiques showrooms, law offices and small businesses. The 1866 Hotaling Building (445–451 Jackson Street) was originally a wholesale liquor firm. *Bus: 12 & 15.*

A taste of life at sea on the SS *Balclutha*

Japantown

The origins of San Francisco's Japanese community date back to the start of the 20th century, when migrants working in the Hawaiian sugar plantations moved on to the fields of California. Many of those that settled here found work in the shipping, retail and art trades, creating several pockets of Japanese life around the city. After the 1906 earthquake, a predominant number moved to the Western Addition, a neighbourhood of Victorian housing west of Van Ness Avenue.

Following the Japanese attack on Pearl Harbor in 1941, many Japanese-Americans were forcibly deported from the city to internment camps. African-American migrants working in the shipyards moved into the Western Addition, and subsequent urban planning has left the heart of today's 12,000-strong Japanese community in a box of streets by the northeast corner of Geary Boulevard and Fillmore Street.

Japan Center

The focus of Japantown is the Japan Center, a five-acre shopping and entertainment complex opened in 1968. It has little of the hectic colour of Chinatown's crowded alleys, but does offer an agreeable taste of Japanese culture in concentrated form. As it is mostly indoors, this is the sort of sight many tourists only get round to if it's raining.

The pivotal point is the 30.5m (100-ft) **Peace Pagoda**, a gift from the people of Japan and a backdrop for the Cherry Blossom Festival held here every April. As well as bookstores, art galleries,

The Peace Pagoda in the Japan Center is a focal point for the city's Japanese community

antiques shops and *sushi* bars, the Center includes the Kabuki Springs & Spa, offering communal Japanese baths, *shiatsu* massage, spa treatments, the Kabuki Theatres (being converted into an art film venue by Robert Redford's Sundance Cinemas), and a variety of Japanese and Korean restaurants.
Post and Buchanan Sts, Geary Blvd. Japan Center Information tel: (415) 922 6776. Open: daily. Bus: 2, 3, 4, 38.

Contemporary Jewish Museum

The museum holds exhibitions on all aspects of historical and contemporary Jewish culture, and fosters links with Israel and Jewish communities throughout the world.
121 Steuart St. Tel: (415) 344 8880; www.jmsf.org. Admission charge. Metro: Embarcadero. Bus: 14. (Call for hours.)

Lombard Street

San Francisco's hills have given rise to 'The World's Crookedest Street'. Its eight curves snake down through flowerbeds in the space of a single block, and provide a favourite location for films, commercials and photo opportunities. The street is only open to descending traffic, with a staircase beside for pedestrians.

Lombard St between Hyde and Leavenworth sts.
Cable car: Powell/Hyde.

National Maritime Museum

An exquisite architectural gem, this sleek 1939 building standing on the south side of Aquatic Park forms part of the San Francisco Maritime National Historical Park (*see p89*). It was designed by William M Mooser Jr to resemble a luxury liner and comes complete with streamlined decks, porthole windows and ship's-wheel door handles. Inside are serene Art Deco murals of Atlantis's underwater life by Hilaire Hiler.

The building's original function was as the 'Aquatic Park Casino', a bathing station for Aquatic Park. Today it houses a maritime museum with exhibits recalling San Francisco's seafaring past from the hearty era of whaling and Cape Horners to the prim days of steamships, yachting and commuting by ferryboat. Panoramic photos upstairs offer an engrossing comparison of the city in the 1850s and 1976.

North end of Polk St at Beach St.
Tel: (415) 447 5000;
www.nps.gov/safr/local/mus.html
Open: daily 10am–5pm.
Free admission.
Cable car: Powell/Hyde. Bus: 19.

The National Maritime Museum looking out over the waters of Aquatic Park

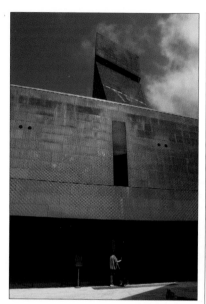
Entrance to the MH de Young Museum in Golden Gate Park

MH de Young Memorial Museum

We have Michael Harry de Young, editor of the *San Francisco Chronicle*, to thank for this fine art museum in Golden Gate Park. It was founded with profits from the 1894 California Midwinter International Exposition that he promoted in the park. The collection opened in 1919, displaying works exhibited in the Exposition, and over the decades it has gathered together a substantial treasury of art from around the world.

The de Young Museum, as it is known locally, reopened copper-clad in a new building on the Music Concourse in Golden Gate Park in late 2005.

Along with the California Palace of the Legion of Honor, the de Young is one of two designated San Francisco Fine Arts Museums. With its modernistic architecture, a 44-m (144-ft) tall pyramid with a free 360° observation platform atop, large sculptures embedded in the landscape, and a terrarium-type fern garden lining a staircase, it holds art that creates a 'survey' museum, that is, one that holds what the other city museums didn't claim or hoard. African, American Indian and Oceania collections, along with textile art and costume collections, were left – and Rockefeller family donations of American paintings, plus a recent gift of one of the world's most extensive New Guinea artefact assemblages, make the eclectic collections more coherent and less regionally parochial than those in the previous Egyptian-Spanish building. Two restored 1894 sphinxes gaze onto Hagiwara Tea Garden Drive near the Pool of Enchantment in the children's garden.

50 Hagiwara Tea Garden Drive, Golden Gate Park. Tel: (415) 863 3330; www.thinker.org. Open: Tue–Sun 9.30am–5.15pm (Fri until 8.45pm). Closed: Mon. Admission charge (free first Tue of the month).

Mission District

Named after Mission Dolores (*see p76*), San Francisco's Hispanic neighbourhood offers visitors a complete and vivid immersion in the Spanish-speaking cultures of Mexico and Central and South America. It was here and in the Presidio that the Spanish missionaries and colonists laid the foundations of modern San Francisco. After the gold rush the area was settled by German and Irish immigrants – the present Latino explosion started in the 1960s, and there is a significant gay and lesbian presence.

The Mission is bisected by the longest street in the city, Mission Street – the most enjoyably intense part lies between 16th and 24th streets. In contrast to the orderly and introspective, drive-everywhere mentality that pervades so much of San Francisco, the fog-free streets here are a colourful parade ground thick with chat, fashion and play. Every shop, bar and *taqueria* proclaims its allegiance to the mother country – Argentine football shirts are on sale next to Guatemalan textiles, Cuban cocktails vie with Mexican *burritos*, a few pavements are even decorated with saucy red and blue

tiles. The Mission's restaurant scene is eclectic – from films projected on a wall at the French Cinema to it-could-be-Ireland pubs.

Part of the excitement of the Mission comes from its colourful and dramatic murals, which invariably have a social or political message to expound. **Balmy Street**, south of 24th Street between Treat and Harrison streets, is a typical example. This was the site of the neighbourhood's first community mural, painted in 1973, and has vivid pictures on the theme of 'Peace in Central America'. There are now some 200 murals in the Mission – the best way to enjoy them is to take a guided tour (*see pp28–9*).
BART: 16th St, 24th St.
Bus: 12, 14, 14L, 26.

Eat, drink and go Hispanic in the Mission, the city's oldest and liveliest neighbourhood

Mission Dolores: today a wedding-cake basilica dwarfs the original adobe-walled mission

Mission Dolores

The Misión San Francisco de Asís is where the story of San Francisco begins. Dedicated to St Francis of Assisi, it was founded on 29 June 1776 by Father Francisco Palou, a student and colleague of Junípero Serra, the creator of the California Missions. He was travelling as part of a Spanish colonising expedition of 34 families led by Juan Bautista de Anza – the Presidio (*see p87*) was established at the same time. The Mission's popular name results from a long-gone nearby lagoon known as Nuestra Señora de los Dolores (Our Lady of the Sorrows).

Mission Chapel

Constructed by Indians, the present Mission building was originally completed in 1791. Its adobe walls are 1.2m (4ft) thick and made from an estimated 36,000 sun-dried bricks. The three bells are Mexican and date from the 1820s. The interior of the chapel is simple but colourful – the patterned design on the beamed ceiling is of Indian origin, while the late 18th-century altar screen was brought from Mexico. Further artefacts from the Mission era are displayed in a small museum by the garden entrance, originally the Mission schoolroom.

Stained glass depicting the Mission chain

Basilica

Rearing up beside the Mission Chapel like a monster kid brother who just discovered fashion, the Basilica was built between 1913 and 1918 to replace the previous church destroyed in the 1906 earthquake. It is decorated in neo-Churrigueresque style, imitating Spanish baroque at its most exuberant, and has windows depicting the 21 Californian Missions.

Cemetery

The harsh truth behind the romantic history of San Francisco is told by the tombstones in this graveyard. Many of its dead are Irish, buried at pitifully young ages in the late 19th century, and others from France, England and South America bear witness to the false hopes of immigration. Other plots belong to the victims of the vigilante gangs, self-elected lawmen who dealt out summary justice in 1850s San Francisco. In their midst a statue of Father Junípero Serra looks down at his weary feet, while another of the maiden Tekakwitha honours the thousands of nameless native American Indians buried in the area. Many were killed by measles, a virus imported by the settlers.
16th & Dolores Sts. Tel: (415) 621 8203.
Open: daily 9am–4.30pm (till 4pm in winter). Admission charge.
Metro: J. Bus: 22, 33.

Museum of the African Diaspora (MoAD)

This SOMA museum of African heritage and its dispersal around the world uses interactive computers to explain the African origins of foods like peanuts

The Mission line

Mission Dolores was the sixth of 21 Missions founded by the Spanish in California. The first was founded in 1769 in San Diego and the last at Sonoma in 1823. Their founding Father was the Mallorca-born Junípero Serra, who was beatified by the Catholic Church in 1988. The Mission line was linked by El Camino Real (The Royal Road) – Highway 82 now follows it north from San Jose to San Francisco. The Missions, along with the Presidios built here and in Monterey and Santa Barbara, were used to convert the native Indians and secure California for the Spanish Crown.

(groundnuts) and coffee, music and clothing styles. There is a narration about slave transportation to the New World, but the museum avoids permanent exhibits in favour of changing theme exhibits such as two-million-year-old stone tools lent by the British Museum and displays by contemporary Black and African American artists.
685 Mission Street at Third St. Tel: (415) 358 7200; www.moadsf.org
Open: Mon, Wed, Fri & Sat 10am–6pm, Thur 10am–9pm, Sun noon–5pm.
Closed: Tue. Admission charge. BART: Montgomery, Powell Stations.
Bus: 14, 15, 30, 45.

Museum of Craft and Folk Art

Northern California's only folk art museum is across the lane from the Four Seasons Hotel and behind the San Francisco Downtown Marriott Hotel. Since its move in late 2005 from Fort Mason, the museum has hosted temporary exhibitions spanning Scandinavian modernists to African American quilt makers. Enticing,

colourful local California craftwork, glass, jewellery and ceramics in the museum store window catch the eye.
51 Yerba Buena Lane between Third and Fourth Sts. Tel: (415) 227 4888; www. mocfa.org. Open: Tue–Fri 11am–6pm, Sat–Sun 11am–5pm. Closed: Mon. Admission charge. BART/Metro: Powell. Bus: 1, 5, 9, 14, 15, 30, 38.

Union Bank of California Museum

The Bank of California was built in 1908 with all the sober, monumental classicism that a temple to moneymaking could muster in a post-earthquake city. Rows of Corinthian columns fence in its great banking hall, beneath which lies a small basement museum devoted to the money that won over the West. Displays include gold nuggets, historic banker's orders, commemorative medals, ingots, banking accessories and exhibits associated with the Comstock silver mines.
Downstairs, 400 California St at Sansome St. Tel: (415) 765 3434 (info). Open: Mon–Fri 9am–4.30pm. Free admission. Cable car: California St. Bus: 1.

Nob Hill

One of the most prestigious addresses in America, Nob Hill's reputation as a luxury residential neighbourhood owes much to the invention of the cable car. Prior to that the rich hogged the best level ground while the poor clambered up the hillsides. After the opening of the California Street line in 1878, this 115-m (376-ft) peak overlooking the Financial District became both accessible and desirable.

By 1882, as Robert Louis Stevenson noted, it was a place where 'millionaires are gathered together vying with each other in display'. Its king was Leland Stanford, who along with Mark Hopkins, Charles Crocker and Collis P Huntington ('The Big Four') invested in the construction of the Central Pacific Railroad. Running east from Sacramento to link with the Union Pacific Railroad at Utah, this pioneered a transcontinental transport link, completed in 1869, which secured their fortunes.

The 1906 earthquake erased their showy castles, but the legacy of these powerful men lives on. Three grand

Pacific Union Club atop Nob Hill, originally the Flood Mansion.

hotels now hoist their names into the skies – the Inter-Continental Mark Hopkins, the Renaissance Stanford Court and the Huntington Hotel – while Grace Cathedral (*see p66*) stands on the site of Crocker's mansion. In their midst stands one haughty survivor, the cocoa-coloured Pacific Union Club (1000 California Street). An exclusive gentlemen's club, it was built in 1886 for James Flood. He belonged to another wealthy quartet, the Irish 'Bonanza Kings' who reaped the profits of the 'Big Bonanza' vein of silver ore discovered in the Virginia City Comstock mines. Memorabilia from the days of Nob Hill's silver and railroad barons can be seen in The Big Four Restaurant at the Huntington Hotel (1075 California Street).
Cable car: Powell/Hyde, Powell/Mason, California St.
Bus: 1 & 27.

North Beach

There's no beach at North Beach – that disappeared soon after the gold rush – just one of San Francisco's oldest and most likeable neighbourhoods. Pizza parlours, aromatic cafés and tricoloured flags on the lampposts proclaim it as 'Little Italy', but the feel and history of North Beach are much more variegated. It's been a Hispanic quarter, 'Little Ireland', home to a Russian-Serbian Greek Orthodox church, a red-light district, jazz hotspot, the Beat Generation's training camp – now it's one big eating and drinking party. The best way to crash it is by strolling north-west along Cristòforo Colombo (Columbus Avenue) to Washington Square (*see p80*).

North Beach Museum

On the mezzanine floor of the US Bank, this small museum documents the Irish, Chinese, Italian and Beat Generation influences on North Beach. Photographs of John B Monaco and the hand-written poetry of Lawrence Ferlinghetti help make the past feel human and accessible.
1435 Stockton St at Columbus Ave.
Tel: (415) 391 6210.
Open: Mon–Fri 9am–5pm.
Free admission.

Washington Square

Washington Square is a purely San Francisco green space. Daily performances start with Chinese residents practising their early-morning *tai chi*, followed by a cavalcade of gnarled old Italian men in suits, chirruping schoolchildren, book-devouring sunbathers and poetry-declaiming down-and-outs. Nightfall brings neon lights, packed restaurants and the beacon of nearby Coit Tower.

The charm of the square owes much to the Church of Saint Peter and Saint Paul, dating from 1924, though tellingly, services here are now also conducted in Chinese, Italian, and, once a month, in Latin. On the grass outside is a statue of Benjamin Franklin, and another by the children's playground pays tribute to the city's volunteer fire crews – paid for in 1933 by the fire engine-chaser Lillie Coit (*see p92*).
Bus: 15, 30, 41, 45.

Walk: North Beach

Proudly Italian, North Beach is best known for its restaurants, coffee bars and neon nightlife. Daylight reveals a much more dappled community, gradually succumbing to the benign advances of Chinatown and increasingly nostalgic for the Beat Generation it nurtured in the 1950s. This walk rolls down Columbus Avenue, then climbs Telegraph Hill for classic views over the city. (*See also p79.*)

Allow 1½ hours, excluding time spent in bars and cafés, which could add a couple of days.

Start from the Transamerica Pyramid at Montgomery and Columbus.

1 Columbus Avenue

From the Transamerica Pyramid (*see p93*), walk northwest up Columbus

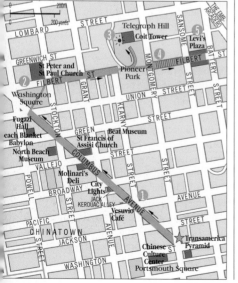

Avenue to pass the 1909 flatiron building that was the earlier home of the Transamerica Corporation. Cross Jackson Street, Kearny Street and Pacific Avenue, passing the fringes of Chinatown. Look out on the left for the Vesuvio Café and City Lights Booksellers at Nos 255 and 261, both hangouts for Beat poets in the 1950s and now divided by Jack Kerouac Alley.

The junction with Broadway, overseen by a vast mural romanticising North Beach life, marks the sleazy corner of the neighbourhood. After crossing Grant Avenue and Vallejo Street, you meet the St Francis of Assisi Church, followed by a gregarious parade of Italian restaurants, delicatessens and cafés, where it would be rude not to stop for at least a coffee. If you ever get to Green Street, take a last look back to the skyscrapers of Downtown, then follow Columbus Avenue as it rolls gently down towards the sea.

Cross Union St and turn right into Washington Square.

2 Washington Square

One of the best places to sit and watch San Francisco go by, the square is lit up by the 1924 St Peter and St Paul Church, a focal point for San Francisco's Italian-American community.

Cross to the northeast corner of Washington Square to climb up Filbert Street. A stiff but short climb culminates in steps to the top of Telegraph Hill.

3 Telegraph Hill

Follow the road upwards for Coit Tower and its splendid murals and panoramic views (*see pp92–3*).

Return to the original route and continue left down Filbert St Steps.

4 Filbert Street Steps

Superb views out to Treasure Island and the Bay Bridge accompany the descent to the sea. The very individual houses and cottages lining these steps exemplify how pockets of country living survive in the midst of the city. As you cross Montgomery Street, No 1360 is a splendid 1936 Art Deco building with etched glass depicting deer, clouds and waves, and silver reliefs. Humphrey Bogart and Lauren Bacall used this location in the 1947 crime film *Dark Passage.*

Continue down the wooden steps, then cross Sansome St into Levi's Plaza.

5 Levi's Plaza

Designed in 1982, the plaza houses the headquarters of Levi Strauss & Co, purveyors of the world-famous denim jeans, first manufactured in the gold rush. If you are here during office hours, have a look at the period examples displayed on the foyer's History Wall. At the opposite corner of the plaza, the Italian restaurant and bakery Il Fornaio is a good place to recover from your mountaineering.

The leafy wooden steps of Filbert Street

Octagon House

Offering plentiful daylight, the
octagonally shaped house exemplifies a
minor architectural fad that provoked
some interest in Victorian San
Francisco. This 1861 example houses a
collection of colonial and federal-era
furniture, antiques and ephemera.
2645 Gough St at Union St.
Tel: (415) 441 7512. Open: second &
fourth Thur and second Sun of every
month, noon–3pm. Donation requested.
Bus: 41 & 45.

Old US Mint

Known as the 'Granite Lady', this
financial fortress in neoclassical disguise
was constructed between 1869 and 1874
and proved sufficiently strong to survive
the 1906 earthquake. Silver and gold
coinage was minted here until 1937. The
San Francisco Museum and Historical
Society has undertaken to restore the
Old Mint for its new role as the
permanent home of the Museum of the
City of San Francisco, currently at
Pier 45.
88 Fifth and Mission Sts, SOMA.
www.sfhistory.org. Closed to public.
Metro: Powell. Bus: 14, 14L, 26, 27.

Pacific Heritage Museum

The museum celebrates the contribution
of the nations of the Pacific Rim to the
West with both changing and
permanent exhibits. Its building forms
part of the Bank of Canton of California
and was originally the 1875 US
Subtreasury, from which some original
features survive. Displays are of a high
quality and might cover subjects such as
Thai costume, Chinese bronzes or the

The Palace of Fine Arts is a survivor of the
buildings created for the Panama-Pacific
Exposition

decorative traditions inspired by
Buddhism. One room is given over to
'Wings over the Pacific', featuring
historic models of Boeing aircraft used
on trans-Pacific routes.
United Commercial Bank, 608
Commercial St. Tel: (415) 399 1124.
Open: Tue–Sat 10am–4pm.
Free admission. Bus: 1, 15, 41.

Palace of Fine Arts

Perhaps the eeriest of San Francisco's
historic sights, this wilfully melancholy
colonnade and rotunda are a legacy of
the 1915 Panama-Pacific International
Exposition. Ostensibly held to celebrate
the opening of the Panama Canal linking
the Pacific and Atlantic Oceans, the 10-
month event also announced the return
of the city to the world scene after the

devastation of the 1906 earthquake.

While Europe descended into the blood and mud of World War I, San Francisco's Marina District became a party-box of national pavilions and funfair amusements. The centrepiece of the 257-hectare (635-acre) site was a glittering Tower of Jewels, decorated with thousands of cut-glass coloured beads and mirrors. Other exhibits included a working model of the Panama Canal and palatial halls devoted to worthy themes like Machinery, Horticulture and Education.

The Palace of Fine Arts was designed by Bernard Maybeck and stood at the west end of the Exposition. Built in neo-classical style with classical columns, a reflective pool and cypresses, it was intended to evoke the dream-like grandeur of Roman ruins – the nymphs apparently checking the state of the roof reflect the sadness of 'life without art'. Though only built as a temporary structure, this much-loved monument survived until the 1960s, when a donation by a local resident enabled it to be permanently reinforced with concrete.

The adjacent exhibition hall now houses the Exploratorium (*see p52*). *Marina Blvd and Baker St. Open access. Bus: 28, 29, 30, 43.*

Pier 39

The big tourist magnet in Fisherman's Wharf (*see*

p53), this fun-for-all wooden-planked pier has two levels of more than 100 cheek-by-jowl shops, restaurants and entertainments. With a carousel, street performers, toy shops and fast-food outlets, it is particularly pleasing to children. Motorised cable-car city tours and Bay cruises with the Blue & Gold Fleet and Red and White Fleet also depart from the piers to the west. The most baffling thing about Pier 39 is the decision of up to 900 California sea lions (billed as 'sea-lebrities') to sunbathe on the decks of its abandoned west-side marina. The Aquarium of the Bay (*see p35*) is on its east side.
The Embarcadero at Beach St.
Tel: (415) 981 7437; www.pier39.com
Shops open daily: 10am–8pm, longer in summer. Free admission.
Metro: F-Line. Bus: 10, 39 & 47.

It's all right for some: sea lions basking in the sun at Pier 39

Painted ladies

In the second half of the 19th century San Francisco grew from a gold-diggers' tented city to a metropolis, as Rudyard Kipling found it in 1899, of 'thousands and thousands of little houses made of wood, each house just big enough for a man and his family'.

Abundant timber in the forests of the Bay Area provided the raw material for this new city, and advances in carpentry and construction methods enabled the mass production of a richly decorated terraced housing that is today collectively termed Victorian. Forty-eight thousand such houses were built

between 1850 and 1915, and despite the fires following the 1906 earthquake and unsympathetic home improvements carried out in later decades, many 'painted ladies' survive as matronly examples of this architectural heritage.

While stylistic diversity is a hallmark, Victorians fall into three predominant groups. Those built during the 1870s are often termed 'Italianate' for their use of classical designs derived from the Italian Renaissance. They have flat roofs with detailed cornices, windows and door frames, and some have angular bay windows. The need for economical land use meant that many Victorians had to fit into a regular plot measuring 7.5m by 30.5m (25ft by 100ft), and they often had similar floor plans. Elaborately painted and ornamented façades were therefore a main source of social distinction.

In the next decade the 'Stick' (also known as Eastlake) style prevailed.

Named after Charles Eastlake, an English furniture designer, this emphasised verticality and is characterised by false gable roofs and square-sided bay windows.

During the 1890s a third style, known as Queen Anne, was imported from the East Coast. These buildings also favoured gable roofs but incorporated elaborate asymmetrical designs such as a corner tower, rounded bay windows and decorative wooden shingles or patterned panels.

Painted ladies love to wear gaudy colours.
Facing page: elaborate bay windows
This page: ornate entrance porches

Presidio

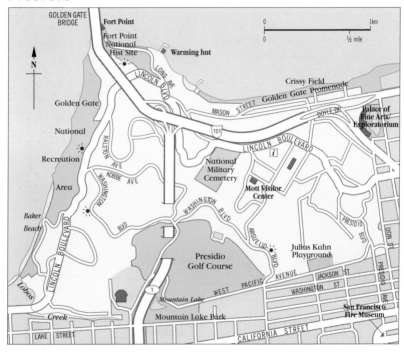

Portsmouth Square

With its early-morning *tai chi* sessions, gaggles of chess and card-players and a children's playground bubbling with young life, Portsmouth Square has

Memorial to Robert Louis Stevenson

become the social focus of Chinatown (*see pp44–5*). An underground car park lies beneath its oppressive concrete, which can attract phenomenal queues at weekends when San Francisco's Chinese-American community returns to its roots to shop and dine. A memorial pays tribute to the Scottish author Robert Louis Stevenson, who lived in the city between 1879 and 1880, and liked to sit here and watch life go by.

Now lorded over by the Hilton San Francisco Financial District Hotel, it is hard to imagine what the square was like when it was the hub of Yerba Buena, the fledgling waterside settlement that preceded San Francisco. The community of 'Good Herb' officially dates from

1835, when an English sailor, William Richardson, built a house on what is now Grant Avenue. American settlers came to join him, mixing with the Californios (California-born Mexicans) who had moved north in the wake of the Spanish colonists. On 9 July 1846, following the United States declaration of war against Mexico, the USS *Portsmouth* sailed into Yerba Buena Cove and hoisted the Stars and Stripes in this plaza. The Mexican forces in the Presidio surrendered peacefully, and six months later Yerba Buena was renamed San Francisco.
Kearny and Washington sts. Bus: 1 & 15.

View down the Parade Ground, Presidio

Presidio of San Francisco

The Presidio (fort) was founded by the Spanish in 1776 and until 1994 was the longest continuously operating military post in the US. In that year, as part of defence cuts ordered by Congress five years previously, its verdant and historic 599 hectares (1,480 acres) were handed over to the National Park Service. Today the Presidio is part of the Golden Gate National Recreation Area, groomed to be 'A Park for the 21st Century'. The good intentions are that its military heritage will be preserved, its forests and shores opened up to public access, and its buildings given over to worthy cultural and educational institutions – all under private administration by 2025.

Mott Visitor Center

With the park still evolving, and under joint administration by the National Park Service and the Presidio Trust (*tel: (415) 561 5300; www.presidio.gov*), the best way to enjoy the Presidio is to contact its William Penn Mott Jr Visitor Center, temporarily in the former officers' club. This is the heart of the military complex. An historic parade ground, where troops mustered for inspection for over two centuries, lies to the north. As well as providing guides and maps detailing the Presidio's buildings and nature trails, you can learn about the excellent weekend programme of escorted walks, hikes and bike rides that unravel its military past.

The architecture of the Presidio is particularly interesting – some wooden buildings survive from the Civil War era, others are tricked out in 1910s Spanish Colonial style, and an original row of 1921 Pilots' Houses, built for the pioneering aviators of nearby Crissy Field, stands near the junction of Lincoln Boulevard and Long Avenue. There are also coastal defence batteries to explore and curiosities like the Pet Cemetery, created in 1945 for guard

dogs but now a shrine to the family pet.
Main gate at Lombard and Lyon sts.
William Penn Mott Jr Presidio Visitor
Center. Tel: (415) 561 4323;
www.nps.gov/prsf. Open: daily 9am–5pm.
Golden Gate Transit. Bus: 28, 29, 43, 82X.

Crissy Field

One of the most popular sections of the
Presidio, Crissy Field is a windy, tidal
marsh that looks much as it did a
century ago – except for the graceful
bayfront promenade, picnic areas and
lush meadows. The original Crissy Field,
a 40.5-hectare (100-acre) US Army
airfield covered with concrete, asphalt,
and chain-link fencing, was removed in
the late 1990s.

The Golden Gate Promenade is part
of the 644-km (400-mile) long Bay Trail,
a shoreline path for walking, running
and wandering. A separate path keeps
cyclists and pedestrians apart. The
windy waters just off Crissy Field are a
world-class boardsailing destination,
well clear of the main shipping channels
beneath the Golden Gate Bridge and
buffeted by steady, dependable breezes
most days of the year.
Along the bay between the Palace of Fine
Arts and Fort Point. Tel: (415) 561 7690.
www.crissyfield.org. Open: daily.
Free admission. Bus: 28, 29, 43.

Russian Hill

Working south from Alaska, Russian fur
traders visited the coast of California at
the same time as the Spanish were
establishing their line of Missions. In
1812 a Russian hunting post was set up
at Fort Ross, 97km (60 miles) north of
San Francisco, and four years later a

Is it a bishop's hat or a half-buried bomb about
to explode? No, it's St Mary's Cathedral

visiting artist, Ludovic Chloris, painted
detailed scenes of native Indians dancing
outside Mission Dolores.

Russian Hill is thought to be so-
named because it was where these
Russian traders buried their dead. With
superb views of the city and Bay, it is
today as desirable a residence as Nob
Hill next door, but has little of its
ostentatious glitz. Here the atmosphere
is one of affluent bohemia – one-off
houses with roof terraces, steep wooded
steps overgrown with ivy, and a creative
population. Literary San Franciscans
such as Ambrose Bierce, Frank Norris,
Ina Coolbrith (honoured with a park)
and Jack Kerouac have resided here, as
well as the architect Willis Polk.
The southern summit of Russian Hill is by
Russian Hill Place, at the junction of
Jones and Vallejo Sts.
Cable car: Powell/Hyde. Bus: 41 & 45.

St Mary's Cathedral

With its hilltop site, vast plaza and
parabolic white walls sweeping up to 58m

(190ft) the Cathedral of Saint Mary of the Assumption is a classic example of the way the architects of modern churches seek to provide spiritual uplift through daring structural engineering and innovative decorative symbolism. Built in 1971, its interior can seat a 2,500-strong congregation and has the feel of a heaven-bound rocket ship. Abstract stained glass represents the four elements, but the eye is first caught by a space-age baldachin suspended above the altar like silver rain, designed by Richard Lippold.
1111 Gough St at Geary St.
Tel: (415) 567 2020;
www.sfarchdiocese.org/cathedral.html
Open: daily, but access restricted during services. Free admission. Bus: 38.

San Francisco Fire Museum

Part of a working fire station in Pacific Heights, this enthusiastic collection of fire-fighting memorabilia includes several historic engines that wouldn't seem out of place in a silent movie. Early hydrants and extinguishers, helmets and uniforms, bugles and badges are accompanied by dramatic photographs of early conflagrations and volunteer crews.
655 Presidio Ave at Pine St.
Tel: (415) 563 4360;
www.sffiremuseum.org
Open: Thur–Sun 1–4pm.
Free admission. Bus: 1, 2, 4, 43.

San Francisco Maritime National Historical Park

Offering insights into the maritime history of San Francisco, the park includes the Hyde Street Pier and the Maritime Museum (*see individual entries*).
Tel: (415) 561 7100; www.nps.gov/safr

The steam-powered tugboat *Hercules* at Hyde Street Pier

Exterior of San Francisco Museum of Modern Art with Caffè Museo to the left

San Francisco Museum of Modern Art (SFMOMA)

In 1995 SFMOMA moved from the Civic Center to new galleries across from the Yerba Buena Gardens, designed by the Swiss architect Mario Botta. The museum is now only second to New York's MOMA in the space it can devote to exhibiting modern art, and has already proved its determination to be at the cutting edge of cultural debate. You might be shocked by what you see, but you won't be disappointed.

Galleries are on four levels and combine travelling shows with a rotating selection from SFMOMA's considerable collection of quality modern art and sculpture. Smart picture-gazers will take the lift to the top and work down. Space is also given to photography, architecture, film and special projects, and there is a well-stocked Museum Store and Caffè Museo.

SFMOMA Collection

In the 60 years prior to this triumphant relocation, SFMOMA has acquired works by many of the leading artists of the 20th century, some of which will always be on view. European masters represented include Picasso, Cézanne and Matisse, whose 1905 *Femme au Chapeau* is probably the most renowned painting in the museum. Paul Klee, American Abstract Expressionists like Jackson Pollock and Clyfford Still, and the work of contemporary Bay Area artists are other fine art strengths.

The photography collection includes work by leading Americans such as Alfred Stieglitz, Imogen Cunningham, Ansel Adams and the European Surrealists. In a city of stunning architecture, it is natural that the likes of Bernard Maybeck (designer of the Palace of Fine Arts), Willis Polk, Frank Lloyd Wright and Timothy Pfleuger are represented, while an entire room created by the furniture designers Charles and Ray Eames is one of the museum's most interesting acquisitions. *151 3rd St (between Mission & Howard Sts). Tel: (415) 357 4000; www.sfmoma.org Open: Fri–Tue 10am–5.45pm (till 8.45pm on Thur). Closed: Wed. Admission charge (free first Tue of every month, half price on Thur 6–9pm). Metro: Montgomery. Bus: 9, 12, 14, 15, 30, 45, 76.*

San Francisco Zoo

At the southern end of Ocean Beach, the grounds of San Francisco Zoo cover a 50.5-hectare (125-acre) site. Opened in 1929, it works hard to be a modern-thinking city zoo providing optimum conditions for both visitors and residents. The range of species of birds and mammals is vast, but the Primate Discovery Center and the quasi-human citizens of Gorilla World are particular favourites. Koala Crossing and Penguin

Island are other popular spots, while Big Cat Feeding (2pm daily except Mon) allows close inspection of lunching lions and tigers. A **Children's Zoo** offers hands-on interaction with farm animals and nature trails. Five species live in the Lipman Family Lemur Forest. The African Savanna and the Great Ape Forest are recent additions.
Sloat Blvd at 47th Ave. Tel: (415) 753 7083; www.sfzoo.org
Open: daily 10am–5pm.
Children's Zoo: 11am–4pm (longer summer hours). Admission charge for adults and children over 2 years old (free first Wed of every month). Metro: L. Bus: 18 & 23.

Mural art
Murals have become a feature of San Francisco's artistic heritage. The colourful frescoes of the Mexican painter Diego Rivera (1886–1957) bedeck walls in the former Pacific Coast Stock Exchange, City Club, San Francisco Art Institute and City College, where a vast Panamerican Mural commissioned for the 1939 Golden Gate International Exposition depicts leading figures from the 1930s. The influence of his bold, social realist style can be seen in the Depression-era murals in Coit Tower, and in the vivid political comment of contemporary street murals in the Mission district. Tours are arranged by City Guides (*see p28*) and the muralists (*tel: (415) 285 2287; www.precitaeyes.org*).

The San Francisco Museum of Modern Art with Art Deco-style office tower rising behind

Telegraph Hill is crowned by the Coit Tower

Telegraph Hill

With commanding views over the Bay, and sometime home to Mark Bitther's wild parrot friends, this hill was the site of a semaphore erected in 1850 to signal the arrival of ships.

Quarrying into the sides explains its cliff-like aspects. Today the summit is accessible by road, a steep walk, or Bus 39. (*See* North Beach walk, *pp80–81.*)

Statue of Columbus on Telegraph Hill

Coit Tower

Telegraph Hill would probably be just another park but for Lillie Hitchcock Coit (1843–1929), who had a deep fascination with fires and firemen who were the superheroes of her day. In girlhood she became the mascot of the Knickerbocker Engine Company No 5, and, as an adult, frequently dressed up in uniform to attend the city's blazes. On her death she left a healthy sum intended for 'adding to the beauty of the city', which resulted in Coit Tower.

Inevitably likened to the nozzle of a fire hose, this 64-m (210-ft) tower was completed in 1933. A lift takes visitors to enjoy the views from the top. The interior murals, however, are equally eye-catching and worth viewing. Commissioned as a Public Works Art Project to provide employment during the Depression, they depict life in California with a rich documentary detail, particularly Victor Arnatoff's masterly *City Life*. Their political comment was deemed so strong that the tower was closed during the violent dockers' strike of 1934.

1 Telegraph Hill Blvd. Tel: (415) 362 0808. Open: daily 10am–6pm. Admission charge. Bus: 39. Keep in mind that there is limited parking available, and long queues are inevitable at popular times. To walk up, see p80.

Transamerica Pyramid

This 48-storey, 260-m (853-ft) pyramidal tower is the city's tallest building. When it was completed in 1972 by William Pereira and Associates, it was likened to a 'corporate teepee' and 'a spike driven through from Hell'. Now it is a much-loved city landmark.

The building served as an emblematic headquarters for US operations of the finance and insurance company Transamerica Corporation. Like many modern beat-the-next-earthquake towers, its floors and foundations are designed to move with the tremors rather than resist them.

Art acquisitions are displayed in the foyer, while, outside, the Transamerica Redwood Park provides a 0.2-hectare (^{1}/$_2$-acre) urban refuge and venue for lunchtime concerts.

600 Montgomery St. Tel: (415) 983 4000; www.transamerica.com
Open: Mon–Fri 8.30am–5pm.
Free admission. Concerts usually run June–Sept on Fri at noon; call to confirm. Bus: 1, 15, 41.

Once ridiculed, the Transamerica Pyramid is now one of the most loved buildings in the city

Treasure Island

Three kilometres (two miles) east of the city, the Island of Yerba Buena provides a stepping stone for the 13.5-km (8$\frac{1}{2}$-mile) San Francisco–Oakland Bay Bridge. Yerba Buena Island has been the property of the US Navy since 1898 and is now partly used by the US Coast Guard. To its north is Treasure Island, a flat, 162-hectare (400-acre) artificial isle built in 1939 to stage the Golden Gate International Exposition, which celebrated the opening of the Bay and Golden Gate Bridges. Treasure Island was scheduled to become San Francisco's airport. With the escalation of World War II it was converted into a naval base. All but deserted during the final decades of the 20th century, Treasure Island was returned to the City of San Francisco in 1997.

During the brief time that Treasure Island functioned as an airport, the 1938 Admiralty Building served as the terminal for Pan American Airways' trans-Pacific China Clipper service – you can still see the old control tower on top of the building. During the 1990s, the Admiralty building was a museum with exhibits about that romantic flying boat link, the 1939 *Exposition*, and the work of the US Navy, Marines Corps and Coast Guard.

Disused hangars and other former military buildings have been reborn as sound stages and studios for San Francisco's film and television industries, while military housing on Yerba Buena Island has been refurbished for civilian use and the port area has become a popular marina.

Much of Treasure Island is still closed to the public, and there are few facilities, so enjoy a picnic on pleasant shoreline

The main administration building on Treasure Island (1939 Golden Gate International Exposition)

Art exhibition and sale held in the new redesigned and reconstructed Union Square

Union Square

Boxed in by top-name department stores and the historic Westin St Francis Hotel, Union Square is the hollow heart of San Francisco. It was redesigned and reopened in 2002 as a broad plaza with arbours, pavilions, an open stage, sculptures and gardens. Union Square, often packed, has coffee, wireless internet access and plenty of concrete steps for lounging or people-watching. It functions like a floral decoration in the centre of a dining table – a bright spot in the midst of major shops, stores and art galleries.

Union Square gets its name from being a rallying point for supporters of the Union in the run-up to the Civil War (1861–5). Today its design masks one of the world's earliest multi-level underground car parks, designed in 1924 by Timothy Pfleuger. At its centre stands a 27-m (90-ft) column commemorating Admiral Dewey's triumph over the Spanish Navy in the Philippines in 1898, topped by a bronze depicting *Victory* (the model, Alma Sprekels, gave the city the Palace of the Legion of Honor Museum).
Powell and Geary sts.
Cable car: Powell/Mason, Powell/Hyde.
Metro: Powell. Bus: 2, 3, 4, 30, 38, 45, 76.

areas with stunning views west toward downtown San Francisco. Best of all, Treasure Island lies west of the Bay Bridge toll plaza, so the drive out and back is free.
Treasure Island, off US-80.
Tel: (415) 274 0660; www.sfgov.org/site/treasureisland.index.asp.
Open: daily during daylight hours.
Free admission. Bus: 108.

Twin Peaks

When it's not foggy, the 360-degree views from this double-summit 278-m (913-ft) hill are stupendous, with San Francisco spread out below like a child's board game. Dream street plans for the city were laid down from a house near this vantage point by the architect Daniel Burnham. After working for two years, he presented his grand project to the city authorities in 1905, only to have it scuppered by the great earthquake of 1906 (*see p56*).
Bus: 37.

View to Yerba Buena Island and Bay Bridge

Financial District office buildings reflected in the window of the Wells Fargo History Museum

Union Street

Once known as Cow Hollow, the stretch of Union Street between Van Ness Avenue and Steiner Street is now a prettified shopping strip fusing the moneyed neighbourhoods of the Marina District and Pacific Heights. Its spruced up Victorians are a rainbow of chic boutiques, bountiful food shops, bijou gift stores, Italian and American restaurants and up-market hangouts for affluent singles. If you like to stroll around small-scale shops with like-minded people, pausing for a drink here and a little purchase there, this is the place.
Bus: 41 & 45.

USS *Pampanito*

Part of the San Francisco Maritime National Historical Park (*see p89*), this US Navy submarine was built in 1943 and made six Pacific patrols during World War II. Clambering around its engine rooms, torpedo bays and confined living quarters gives a frightening insight into life on board. All submarine crews were volunteers, and the contribution to the war made by those who fought beneath the waves aboard 'SS-383' is recalled in an informative self-guided audio tour.

The USS *Pampanito* sank six Japanese ships, including one discovered to have been carrying British and Australian prisoners-of-war. The submarine rescued 73 survivors from the engagement. Today, the vessel is open to the public as a tribute to the thousands of missing submariners 'still on patrol'.
Pier 45, Fisherman's Wharf.
Tel: (415) 775 1943; www.maritime.org/ pamphome.htm. Open: daily 9am–6pm, Fri–Sat to 8pm (longer in summer). Admission charge. Cable car: Powell/ Hyde. Metro: F-Line. Bus: 39 & 47.

Wells Fargo History Museum

Wells, Fargo & Co was founded in 1852 to provide banking and transport services between California and the eastern United States. As this museum emphatically proves, the story of the gold rush and the company's famous stagecoaches are indeed the stuff of Wild West movies. Gold nuggets, scales, miners' lamps and early banknotes bring home the realities of the prospectors' world, while the growth of the 'Golden State' is recorded in exhibits on subjects like the Bear Flag Revolt, the telegraph system, and the exploits of robbers such as Black Bart, who always liked to leave a poem behind after a hold-up.

420 Montgomery St at California St.
Tel: (415) 396 2619;
www.wellsfargohistory.com
Open: Mon–Fri 9am–5pm.
Closed: weekends. Free admission.
Cable car: California St. Bus: 10 & 15.

Yerba Buena Gardens

The building of Yerba Buena Gardens and Yerba Buena Art District has been a crucial factor in the rebirth of the SOMA district (meaning South of Market). Spread over and around the 1981 Moscone Convention Center, it includes the Yerba Buena Center for the Arts, San Francisco Museum of Modern Art, Museum of the African Diaspora, Museum of Craft and Folk Art, the Cartoon Art Museum (*see individual entries*), and Zeum children's centre.

The centre of the complex is laid out with gardens and walkways mined with modern sculpture. On the south side the Martin Luther King Jr Memorial pays tribute to the assassinated civil rights campaigner with a 15-m (50-ft) wide waterfall and panels engraved with his words. On the level above, the Sister Cities Garden incorporates plants from San Francisco's 13 sister cities, which range from the Irish city of Cork and Abidjan, capital of the Ivory Coast, to Sydney, Australia.

Mission St at 3rd & 4th sts. Tel: (415) 541 0312; www.yerbabuena.org
Metro: Powell. Bus: 9X, 14X, 15, 30, 45.

The USS *Pampanito*, a World War II submarine, is open to the public

Walk: downtown

This walk plunges into the heart of San Francisco, an intense grid of streets crammed with department stores, office and hotel complexes and the sublime skyscrapers of the Financial District. Time the walk for a weekday, when the Financial District is in full swing.

Allow 1 hour.

The walk starts in Hallidie Plaza, at the junction of Powell and Market streets. From the urban stage of the cable-car turnaround, walk north up Powell Street to Union Square.

1 Union Square

Bounded by the Westin St Francis hotel and leading department stores, the square is named after the pro-Union rallies held here in the days of the Civil War (*see p95*).

Leave the square at its southeast corner, crossing the road to walk north up Stockton Street. Turn right into Maiden Lane.

2 Maiden Lane

With its designer shops, art galleries and tables and chairs set out for lunching executives, Maiden Lane bears little resemblance to the notorious street of brothels that flourished here until the 1906 earthquake. The Xanadu Gallery at No 140 was designed in 1948 by Frank Lloyd Wright.

Cross Grant Ave and continue to Kearny St. Turn left, then right down Post St to enter the Crocker Galleria.

3 Financial District

Now you are amidst the neck-cricking world of San Francisco's business community. The 1982 glass-vaulted Crocker Galleria takes its cue from the Galleria Vittorio Emanuele in Milan. At its northern end, at 130 Sutter Street, stands the Hallidie Building, designed by Willis Polk in 1918. Framed with ornate

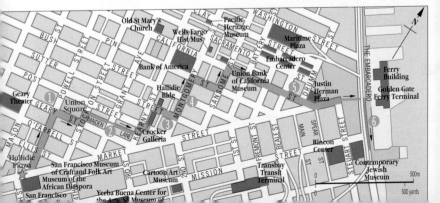

metal cornices, its façade is a pioneering example of the glass curtain wall.
Turn right down Sutter St to reach Montgomery St, then turn left.

4 Montgomery Street
The shore of Yerba Buena Cove ran close to this street before new land was claimed from the sea after the gold rush. The city's first banking street boasts several historic skyscrapers, such as the 1890 Mills Building at No 220 and the 1927 Russ Building opposite at No 235.
Turn right down Pine St to pass the grey former Pacific Coast Stock Exchange Building at No 301, designed by Miller and Pfleuger in 1930. Then turn left at Sansome St and walk to California St.

5 California Street
On the corner is the neoclassical Bank of California, designed in 1908 and now incorporating the Union Bank of California Museum (*see p78*).
Turn right to walk the length of California Street.

With its cable-car line climbing up to Nob Hill, the street has always been a prestigious address. The Tadich Grill at No 240 retains the atmosphere of old San Francisco. As you near Market Street you will see the Embarcadero Center to the left and the Hyatt Regency San Francisco hotel ahead.
At the junction with Market St turn left towards the Ferry Building.

6 Embarcadero
To the left you will pass Justin Herman Plaza, with its squashed spider fountain designed by Armand Vaillancourt in 1971. In the park to the right is a statue of King Carlos III of Spain. Cross to the Ferry Building (*see p51*) and follow the signs to the right for the Golden Gate Ferry. These end by a quay with superb views of the Bay Bridge.
There are bus stops and Metro/BART: Embarcadero station at the end of Market St.

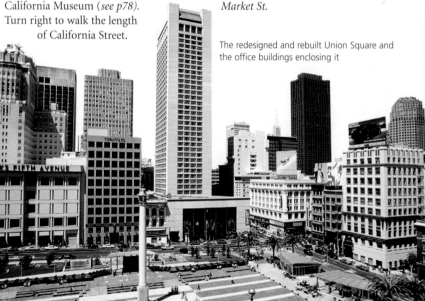

The redesigned and rebuilt Union Square and the office buildings enclosing it

By bus: Ocean Beach

Buses provide a simple and inexpensive way of touring San Francisco. This three-bus circuit travels from Downtown to Ocean Beach to explore the untouristy western half of the city. This route (*see map on pp18–19*) is based on weekday timetables only – you may want to buy a MUNI Passport before setting off (*see p21*).

Allow 2½ hours, excluding time in the zoo.

The bus ride starts at the southwest corner of Union Square, at the junction of Geary and Powell Sts. The 38L bus stop is in Geary St, opposite Lefty O'Doul's restaurant.

Flower-carpeted cliffs of Ocean Beach

1 Union Square to Point Lobos

Board a 38L bus with 'Point Lobos' on the front – and no other! At weekends the 38 bus travels the same route. Running the entire length of Geary Boulevard, 'The Geary' cuts through San Francisco's mixed communities. After the bright lights of Union Square and the Theater District come the rough edges of the Tenderloin and, crossing Van Ness Avenue, a climb up to St Mary's Cathedral and Japantown.

Further west lie the multicultural residential rows of Laurel Heights and the Richmond district – Clement Street, a block further north, is rapidly growing into a second Chinatown. Look out on the right for the gold onion domes of the Russian Orthodox Holy Virgin Cathedral, on the corner of Geary Boulevard and 26th Avenue. The Russian community here dates from an influx of 10,000 immigrants after the 1917 Revolution. *Alight at the junction of Point Lobos and 48th Ave.*

2 Ocean Beach

Walk downhill towards the sea. On the left you pass Sutro Heights Park. This and the ruins of Sutro Baths and the

Cliff House ahead are the legacy of the property tycoon Adolf Sutro (*see p50*). If it's cold and windy, Louis Café, on the right at 902 Point Lobos Avenue, is the best place on the ride for a drink or snack. Continue downhill to enjoy the sands and breezes of Ocean Beach.
Turn left into Balboa St, then right into La Playa St. The 18 bus stop is by Cabrillo St, opposite Safeway.

3 Ocean Beach to San Francisco Zoo

Board an 18 bus. This travels south past the windmills of Golden Gate Park – first the complete Dutch Windmill built in 1902, then the sail-less Murphy Windmill of 1905. Both, now undergoing restoration, were used to pump water for the park up to a reservoir on Strawberry Hill. The bus then continues down 46th Avenue through the low-rise, pastel-toned suburbia of the Sunset District. This residential area developed in the 1930s, providing family homes with garages for the new automobile age. Relentlessly middle class, it is known as the 'Fog Belt' because of the summer fog that engulfs it.
Alight by the entrance to the San Francisco Zoo at Sloat Blvd.

4 Return from L

For the San Francisco Zoo *see pp90–91*. To reach the L Metro stop, taking you back to Downtown, walk north up 46th Avenue to the junction with Wawona Street. The streetcar runs eastward on the surface along Taraval Street as far as West Portal Station, then burrows underground. If you fancy exploring another neighbourhood, take a stroll around the Castro (*see p40*) two stops further on.
The L Metro line continues to Embarcadero. Alight at Powell St station for Union Square.

The Castro – one of San Francisco's more colourful neighbourhoods

By bike: Sausalito

San Francisco's exceptional combination of cityscape, countryside and seashore makes cycling here a pleasure. This leisurely ride runs west from Fisherman's Wharf to cross the Golden Gate Bridge and return by ferry from Sausalito. (*For Blue & Gold Fleet ferry times, call (415) 705 5555. Also visit www.blueandgoldfleet.com*)
Allow 3 hours.

The ride starts by the Hyde Street Pier, at the junction of Hyde and Jefferson Streets.

1 Aquatic Park to Marina Green
Follow the seafront path from Hyde Street Pier west around Aquatic Park.

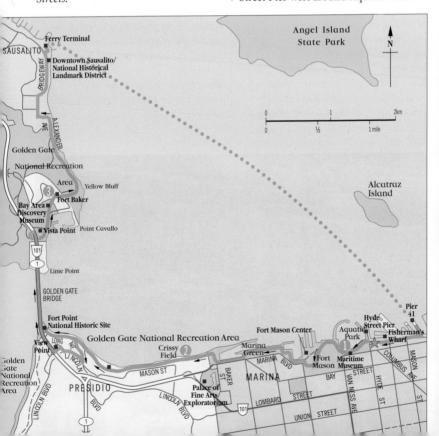

Turn left up a hill, marked 'Bay Trail', towards Fort Mason. Continue into the park, following the red paths past the statue of Congressman Phillip Burton, the environmental campaigner credited with the creation of the Golden Gate National Recreation Area in 1972. Ride downhill past the entrance to the Fort Mason Center, then continue west to the quays of the Marina Small Craft Harbor and the fitness stage of Marina Green.

2 Crissy Field to Golden Gate Bridge

Turn right by Baker Street, passing Il Kiosko to reach the sea. Follow the water's edge to Crissy Field, which served as a military airfield between 1921 and 1936. Continue to reach Fort Point National Historic Site (*see p59*), popular with local fishermen and runners. Spray from the Bay will catch you as you return past Long Avenue uphill to Lincoln Boulevard. Turn right, follow the signs to Golden Gate Bridge. A path leads through the woods to the View Point and entrance to the bridge (*see p60*). *Depending on security and current rules, cyclists may be directed to cross by different sides of the bridge at varying times during the week. If you take the west side, turn left at the far end of the bridge to cycle beneath it and join the coastal road (Conzelman Rd) running east to Fort Baker. If you cross on the east side, take the exit (Alexander Ave) immediately after the Vista Point and follow the brown-and-white signs to the Bay Area Discovery Museum.*

3 (East) Fort Baker to Sausalito

East Fort Baker was part of a complex arsenal of gun batteries and coastal

fortifications built in the first half of this century to protect the Golden Gate, with barracks and quarters nearby for the soldiers who manned them. (*For the* Bay Area Discovery Museum, *see p150.*)

From the parade ground and Coast Guard Station, Fort Baker Road leads north to Sausalito (also marked 'Bay Trail'). Join the main road (Alexander Ave) into Sausalito, marked with green 'Bike Route' signs. This weaves through the town to reach the National Historical Landmark District. Turn right down El Portal to reach the ferry terminal. (*For* Sausalito *see p116.*) *In busy times, bicycles board first and leave last. Return across the Bay to the ferry docks on Fisherman's Wharf. To return to Hyde St turn right and cycle along Jefferson St. The F-Line runs along The Embarcadero for speedy bayfront access to downtown.*

Bikes can be hired nearby from **Bay City Bike** *2661 Taylor St, tel: (415) 346 2453. www.baycitybike.com*

Biking within sight of the Golden Gate Bridge

Tour: 49-Mile Scenic Drive

The 49-Mile Scenic Drive offers a thorough and enjoyable introduction to San Francisco's 122sq km (47sq miles), although the city no longer promotes this tourist driving circuit. Sunday is the best day, on other days avoid the rush-hour traffic.

The drive could be completed in 4 hours, but it is better to devote the best part of a day.

This itinerary starts by the Ferry Building at the junction of the Embarcadero and Market St. The circuit can be picked up at any point and followed anticlockwise.

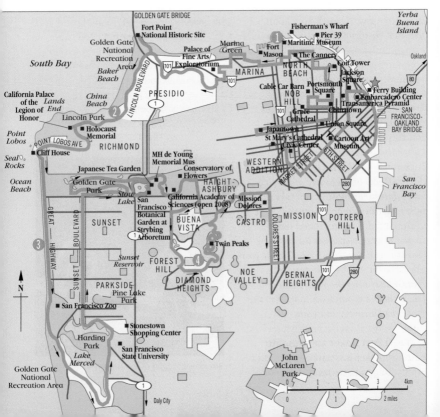

1 Downtown to Fisherman's Wharf

Drive north and turn left into Washington Street, then Battery Street. Continue down to Market Street and on to Howard Street. Turn right and right again on 9th Street. At the Civic Center go north on Larkin Street to Geary Boulevard. Follow the seagulls to loop around Japantown, returning east along Post Street. This leads down to the Financial District and a left turn up Grant Avenue to Chinatown. Turn left up the steep incline of California Street to Nob Hill. The drive continues via Taylor, Washington, Clay and Kearny streets to Columbus Avenue and North Beach. Turn right up Grant Avenue for Telegraph Hill and Coit Tower. This is a good spot to stop for city views (*see p92*). Pick up the route again in Lombard Street and continue to Fisherman's Wharf.

2 Aquatic Park to Cliff House

Follow the coast west via Jefferson, Beach and Bay streets. After passing Fort Mason and Marina Green (look out for the left turn up Scott Street), the drive passes the Palace of Fine Arts and the Presidio. Continue on Lincoln Blvd to view Fort Point and Golden Gate Bridge and return to follow the cliffs. Pass the California Palace of the Legion of Honor Museum and golf course in Lincoln Park and take Point Lobos Avenue to the Cliff House.

3 Ocean Beach to Golden Gate Park

Continue downhill to drive the length of Ocean Beach on the Great Highway, passing San Francisco Zoo to follow John Muir Drive around Lake Merced. Turn left into Lake Merced Boulevard, driving north past Harding Park golf course to take Sunset Boulevard to Golden Gate Park (*see p62*). Road signs direct you through the park to emerge at Stanyan Street.

On Sundays John F Kennedy Drive from 19th Ave to Stanyan St is closed to traffic. Follow the signs for the alternative route along Martin Luther King Jr Drive to exit Golden Gate Park at Stanyan St.

4 Haight-Ashbury to Twin Peaks

Turn right on Parnassus Street. Now follow the seagulls' winding ascent of Twin Peaks via 7th Avenue and Laguna Honda Boulevard. From the summit, unless it is foggy, you can see the city spread out below. The descent cuts between the Haight-Ashbury and the Castro via Roosevelt Way and 14th Street to savour the palm-lined splendour of Dolores Street. If you arrive before 4pm, you could visit Mission Dolores (*see p76*).

Compared to what you have just enjoyed, the rest of the drive hardly merits its 'Scenic' title. But you can continue along Cesar Chavez (Army) St, turning left on to Highway 280 to curl back to the Embarcadero.

Road signs indicate the route of the 49-Mile Scenic Drive

Bridging the Bay

The Golden Gate Bridge and the San Francisco–Oakland Bay Bridge (commonly known as the Bay Bridge) were both opened within six months of each other – a sensational double act born of visionary engineering, the rise of the automobile, and a surge of civic pride that culminated in the Golden Gate International Exposition on Treasure Island in 1939.

Work began on both bridges in 1933, with the 13.5-km (8¹/₂-mile) Bay Bridge opening first in November 1936. It is in fact two bridges: a suspension bridge spanning the waters between the Embarcadero and Yerba Buena Island, and a cantilever section bounding over to the Oakland waterfront that will be rebuilt (bids from construction companies are currently being considered). It carries 280,000 cars a day.

The 2.7-km (1³/₄-mile) Golden Gate Bridge opened in May 1937, and has become a world-famous city emblem that is still a thrill to cross. Its chief architect was Joseph Strauss, who built over 400 bridges. His several assistants are credited with its elegant Art Deco design, which makes light of the monumental construction tasks the bridge required. Sinking the piers on which its two 227-m (746-ft) towers rest was a feat similar to building skyscrapers underwater. Essential trivia: in high winds the roadway can sway up to 8m (27 ft) in the centre; the bridge is forever being painted in a colour known as International Orange; it takes four years to apply a complete coat.

Another three main bridges cross the waters of the Bay. The oldest is the southern Dumbarton Bridge, first built in 1927 but replaced with the present steel skeleton in 1984. In the north is the 9-km (5¹/₂-mile) Richmond–San Rafael Bridge. Connoisseurs of bridge experiences should also seek out the San Mateo-Hayward Bridge, opened in 1967, which links San Mateo and Hayward. Spanning 11km (6³/₄ miles), its eastern section comprises a level slipway that gives a divine feeling that you are driving on water.

Above: surf breaking at Fort Point, just below the Golden Gate Bridge
Facing page: the Golden Gate Bridge, a monument to engineering skills

Around the Bay

The big thrill of the Bay Area is its scenic variety. Even though parts of it are laced with freeways and dormitory conurbations, there are abundant opportunities to lose yourself in nature and have fun. Imperious redwood forests, bountiful wine valleys, wild mountains and soothing country parks, the sandy beaches and breezy headlands of the Pacific coast – all these can be visited comfortably in a day trip from San Francisco.

If you have the time to take things easy, spend a night in the Sonoma Valley or by Highway 1. If time is short, a trip to Muir Woods is instantly refreshing.

Such accessible natural beauty makes a car both essential and desirable, but remember that you can easily take the BART to Berkeley and the ferry to Oakland. If you're heading off to the beaches, woods and parks for the day it's best to have a picnic on board and a full petrol tank.

In the summer potential fire hazards can lead to the closure of backroads and parks, so ring ahead for the latest situation.

View south from the Marin Headlands, north of Golden Gate Bridge

Bay Area (*see p126 for orange route tour*)

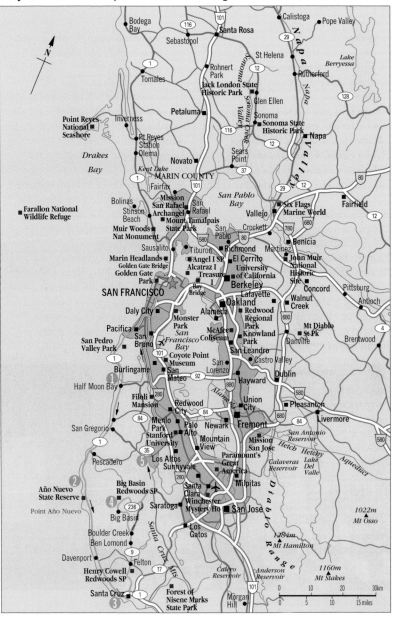

N

Bodega Bay
Calistoga
Pope Valley
116
101
Santa Rosa
29
Sebastopol
St Helena
Lake Berryessa
1
Rohnert Park
12
Rutherford
Tomales
Jack London State Historic Park
128
Glen Ellen
Petaluma
Sonoma
Napa
Point Reyes National Seashore
Inverness
116
Sonoma State Historic Park
Napa Valley
Pt Reyes Station
Olema
Drakes Bay
Novato
Sears Point
12
Kent Lake
MARIN COUNTY
37
80
Fairfax
101
San Pablo Bay
29
12
Farallon National Wildlife Refuge
Bolinas
San Rafael
Six Flags Marine World
Fairfield
Mission San Rafael Arcángel
San Rafael
Vallejo
12
Stinson Beach
Mount Tamalpais State Park
San Pablo
Crockett
780
680
Muir Woods Nat Monument
580
Richmond
Martinez
Benicia
Sausalito
Tiburon
El Cerrito
John Muir National Historic Site
Marin Headlands
Angel I SP
Golden Gate Bridge
Alcatraz I
University of California
Golden Gate Park
Treasure I
Berkeley
Concord
Pittsburg
SAN FRANCISCO
Bay Bridge
Lafayette
Antioch
Oakland
Walnut Creek
Daly City
Monster Park
Alameda
Redwood Regional Park
Mt Diablo St Pk
4
Pacifica
San Bruno
San Francisco Bay
McAfee Coliseum
Knowland Park
680
Danville
Brentwood
San Pedro Valley Park
101
Coyote Point Museum
San Leandro
Castro Valley
1
Burlingame
San Mateo
92
San Lorenzo
Dublin
Half Moon Bay
880
Hayward
580
Filoli Mansion
280
Union City
680
Pleasanton
84
Redwood City
84
Newark
Fremont
Livermore
San Gregorio
Menlo Park
Palo Alto
San Antonio Reservoir
580
1
Stanford University
Mountain View
Mission San Jose
Hetch Hetchy Aqueduct
35
Los Altos
Paramount's Great America
Calaveras Reservoir
Lake Del Valle
Pescadero
Sunnyvale
280
Año Nuevo State Reserve
Big Basin Redwoods SP
Santa Clara
Milpitas
Diablo Range
Point Año Nuevo
236
Winchester Mystery Ho
San Jose
1022m
Mt Osso
Big Basin
Saratoga
Boulder Creek
Los Gatos
1284m
Mt Hamilton
Ben Lomond
Santa Cruz Mts
1160m
Mt Stakes
9
Davenport
Felton
Calero Reservoir
Anderson Reservoir
17
Henry Cowell Redwoods SP
0 10 20 30km
Santa Cruz
1
Forest of Nisene Marks State Park
Morgan Hill
101
0 5 10 15 miles

East Bay

Berkeley

Draped on the ridges of the East Bay, Berkeley has always lived in thrall to 'Cal', the University of California created in 1868 and one of the most famous in America. Its reputation owes much to the wealth and energy of its benefactress Phoebe Hearst, wife of the mining tycoon George Hearst and mother of press baron William Randolph Hearst, who pumped in over $15 million worth of support. Today it has around 33,000 students and a tally of 19 Nobel Laureates.

Campus tours

The 499-hectare (1,232-acre) campus is a brain-soothing parkland with serene lawns and graceful academic buildings. The hushed progress of students between lecture halls and seminar rooms makes it hard to believe that the same university was a hotbed of protest in the 1960s and early 1970s, vehemently supporting the civil rights movement and nationwide demonstrations against the Vietnam War.

A map and guided or DIY tours are available from the Visitor Center at the corner of Oxford Street and University Avenue. A useful early target is the 93.5-m (307-ft) **Sather Tower**, modelled on the bell tower of St Mark's Square in Venice, which offers sweeping views in all directions from an observation platform, and daily carillon concerts.

Other key sights worth seeking out are the aesthetic 1907 **Hearst Mining Building**, the **Bancroft Library**, which has a small museum of Californian history, and Berkeley's traditional meeting and ranting venue, **Sproul Plaza**.
Visitor Information Center: 101

Street scene on Telegraph Avenue, Berkeley

University Hall, 2200 University Ave.
Tel: (510) 642 5215; www.berkeley.edu
Tours leave Mon–Fri at 10am from the
Visitor Information Center, and from
Sather Tower on Sat 10am & Sun 1pm.
Sather Tower Campanile: Open Mon–Fri
10am–4pm, Sat 10am–5pm, Sun
10am–1.30pm, 3–5pm. Admission charge.
Call to verify opening times during
University holidays.

Lawrence Hall of Science

Mainly catering to schoolchildren, this
interactive museum hides in the hills
above the main campus, linked by a
shuttle bus from Hearst Mining Circle.
Exhibits are on science-is-fun themes
like maths around the world, the human
brain and a gravity wall.
Centennial Drive. Tel: (510) 642 5132;
www.lawrencehallofscience.org
Open: daily 10am–5pm.
Admission charge.

Phoebe A Hearst Museum of Anthropology

This small but quality museum displays
changing exhibits from its far-ranging
collection of anthropological and
archaeological treasures. One part tells
the story of Ishi, 'the last Californian
Indian', who came in from the
mountains in 1911 to live in the
museum (then based in San
Francisco) and pass on invaluable
knowledge about the crafts and lore
of his Yahi tribe. He died five years
later from tuberculosis.
103 Kroeber Hall, Bancroft Way at
College Ave. Tel: (510) 642 3682;
http://hearstmuseum.berkeley.edu
Open: Wed–Sat 10am–4.30pm,

Sun noon–4pm.
Admission charge (free on Thur).

Telegraph Avenue

The spirit of the Sixties lives on in the
hippy craft stalls lining Telegraph Avenue
– just. The four blocks that matter run
south from Sproul Plaza to Dwight Way.
Once a nexus of militant protest and
riot, they are now a sad and histrionic
strip where street traders selling tie-dye
shirts and labour-intensive jewellery mix
with drunks, punks and students doing
mundane things like buying books,
stationery and computer gadgetry.

Berkeley Art Museum and Pacific Film Archive

Stimulating and provocative exhibitions
are guaranteed in the spacious art gallery,
which also has a permanent collection
of work by the abstract colourist Hans
Hofmann. The university-based film
archive offers a wide variety of
showings, from classic WC Fields to
experimental documentaries.
Berkeley Art Museum: 2626 Bancroft Way
at College Ave, 2621 Durant Ave.
Tel: (510) 642 0808. Open: Wed–Sun
11am–5pm, Thur to 7pm. Admission
charge (free first Thur of the month).
Pacific Film Archive: 2575 Bancroft Way.
Tel. (510) 642 1124;
www.bampfa.berkeley.edu
Admission charge.

Berkeley is 19km (12 miles) east across
Bay Bridge. BART: Berkeley. Bus: AC
Transit. Berkeley Convention & Visitors
Bureau is at 2015 Center St. Tel: (510)
549 7040, 800 847 4823 (toll-free);
www.visitberkeley.com

Oakland

If you've fallen madly in love with San Francisco, Oakland is like taking the cold but necessary shower. The city is easily reached via the Bay Bridge, but the best introduction is to arrive by ferry, which passes the mammoth docks and naval yards of one of the largest ports on the West Coast. As drugs and crime are a problem in this depressed area, it is best to stick to busy and well-lit streets.

One of Oakland's claims to fame, though, is that it is the home town of Green Day, the hugely successful punk band.

Jack London Waterfront

The ferry from San Francisco berths by Oakland's equivalent to Fisherman's Wharf, named in homage to the writer Jack London (*see p114*). Bear right to reach Jack London Square. Beyond it is the log cabin where he lived while prospecting in the 1897 Klondike Gold Rush.
*Tel: (866) 295 9853;
www.jacklondonsquare.com. Ferry: Blue & Gold from Ferry Building or Pier 41.*

Downtown

From Jack London Square, Broadway runs north under the Nimitz freeway to the architectural miscellany of the city centre. On the right, between 8th and 9th streets, is Oakland's Chinatown, free of the gaudy, tourist-pleasing trappings adopted in San Francisco. Shimmering skyscrapers point to new investment in the heart of the city, but its most poignant buildings are those left from the dream-filled days of the 1930s,

notably the Paramount Theater at 2025 Broadway, designed in 1931 by Timothy Pfleuger. Another eye-catching landmark is the 1923 Tribune Tower on 13th and Franklin streets, home of the *Oakland Tribune* newspaper.
BART: 12th St. Bus: AC Transit.

Oakland Museum of California

A walk east along 11th Street brings you to this functional three-level museum where you could easily spend several hours enjoying a comprehensive account of the ecology, history and art of California. The history galleries are the most engrossing, cruising smoothly from native Indian culture and the gold-crazed 1850s into the modern world of Beats, hippies and computer whizz-kids. A bookstore, cafeteria and rooftop sculpture gardens lighten the burden of self-education.
*1000 Oak St at 10th St.
Tel: (510) 238 2200; www.museumca.org
Open: Wed–Sat 10am–5pm, Sun
noon–5pm. Closed: Mon & Tue.
Admission charge (free on second Sun of
every month). BART: Lake Merritt.*

*Oakland is on the east side of the Bay
Bridge. Oakland Convention & Visitors
Bureau: 463 11th St, Oakland.
Tel: (510) 839 9000;
www.oaklandcvb.com*

Oakland public art: *Sigame/Follow Me* (2001), Scott Donahue

View of new and old architecture in downtown Oakland; the Tribune Tower is centre

North Bay

Jack London State Historic Park

Born in San Francisco, raised in Oakland, Jack London (1876–1916) lived for adventure and writing. At one time the highest paid author in the US, his novels, journalism and short stories dealt in the fundamental human dramas he witnessed during an itinerant life that included prospecting in the Klondike Gold Rush and sailing a ketch to the South Pacific.

In 1911 he and his wife Charmian moved to a 567-hectare (1,400-acre) estate near Glen Ellen that he christened 'Beauty Ranch'. Here he continued writing and supervising the construction of Wolf House, a dream home that mysteriously burned down close to completion. Three years later he died, but his wife continued to stay in a new home, the House of Happy Walls, until 1955. Today this is a faithful museum to London, while part of the ranch is now a tranquil park that includes farm buildings and the writing 'cottage' where he died.

76km (47 miles) north at Glen Ellen. Tel: (707) 938 5216; www.parks.ca.gov Museum open: daily 10am–5pm, park from 8am. Admission charge.

Marin Headlands

A curtain of green hanging on the northwest side of Golden Gate Bridge, the Marin Headlands, part of the Golden Gate National Recreation Area/national park, are a remarkably wild and unspoilt sanctuary for wildlife and de-stressing city victims. The best touring route is clockwise, stopping first at Battery Spencer for a stupendous view back to San Francisco. Continue west along the one-way Conzelman Road. The remains of gun emplace-

Cottage and garden, Jack London State Historic Park

ments along the coast are a legacy of the long military presence here, which also protected the headlands from attack by developers. For more information visit *www.nps.gov/goga/mahe/*

The road winds on west to a stop overlooking Point Bonita Lighthouse, built in 1874. Continue north to the Visitor Center at the east end of Rodeo Lagoon, which occupies the former military chapel. Information is available on the trails, horse riding, birdwatching and beaches to be enjoyed in the area. To return to civilisation drive east along Bunker Road.

Marine Mammal Center

On the north side of Rodeo Lagoon a former missile site is now a hospital-cum-orphanage for seals and sea lions. Volunteers run it and visitors are welcome to observe the mammals' treatment and recuperation.
Tel: (415) 289 7325;
www.marinemammalcenter.org
Open: daily 10am–4pm. Free admission. Donations welcome.

Take the Alexander Ave exit on the north side of Golden Gate Bridge. Visitor Center tel: (415) 331 1540. Open: daily 9.30am–4.30pm. Bus: 76 on Sun only.

Six Flags Marine World

Wildlife shows, an oceanarium and a family fun theme park come together in 65 hectares (160 acres) of animal-packed action. Attractions include Bengal tigers, elephants, chimpanzees, alligators, a walk-in aviary and butterfly habitat, an opportunity to travel through a transparent acrylic tunnel while sharks, rays and tropical fish whizz overhead, and a number of thrilling roller coasters.
48km (30 miles) northeast, in Vallejo via Interstate 80 and Highway 37. Tel: (707) 643 6722. Ferry: Blue & Gold from Pier 39. Tel: (415) 773 1188; www.sixflags.com/parks/marineworld/index.asp. Open: daily in summer, call for timings. Admission charge.

Mount Tamalpais State Park

See p134.

Muir Woods National Monument

Muir Woods National Monument provides many visitors with their first experience of the majesty of redwood trees. Named after John Muir (1838–1914), the champion of forest conservation in the United States, this 199-hectare (491-acre) arboreal heaven lies at the foot of Mount Tamalpais and is a rare example of first-growth coastal redwood forest. An easy trail leads from

Whales are just one of the many natural stars performing at Six Flags Marine World

the Visitor Center around some of its mightiest denizens.

19km (12 miles) north via US 101 and Highway 1. Visitor Center tel: (415) 388 2595; www.nps.gov/muwo. Open: daily 8am–sunset. Admission charge.

Napa Valley

America's premier wine region has become a parade of showcase vineyards where you can spend many merry hours tasting quality wine, picnicking on lawns, ballooning, comparing winery architecture, learning about viticultural processes and admiring fine art and sculpture. Quite a few visitors even come here to buy some wine.

The greatest density of wineries, many of which now produce brand names to equal the best in the world, stretches north along Highway 29 between Napa and Calistoga. Locals will tell you that it's best to only visit a few of them and to avoid the weekends when there are crowds and traffic jams, but no one listens (*see p124*).

76km (47 miles) northeast via US 101.

Point Reyes National Seashore

See pp135.

Sausalito

Welcome to 'The Geneva of America', as a 1910 tourist brochure once boldly described this relaxed and affluent waterfront town. Sausalito's proximity to the Golden Gate Bridge and the Marin Headlands, backed by regular ferry connections to San Francisco, makes it a soft target for tourists taking a trip on the Bay. The views back to the city are marvellous, and there are plenty of bars

and restaurants where you can enjoy a leisurely meal looking out at the boats on the Bay. It can get very crowded at weekends.

13km (8 miles) north. Take Alexander Ave exit from US 101 north of Golden Gate Bridge.
Ferry: Blue & Gold Fleet from Pier 41 or the Ferry Building.
Bus: Golden Gate Transit.

Bay Area Discovery Museum
See p150.

San Francisco Bay and Delta Model
To the north of downtown Sausalito, this enormous and fascinating computer-controlled scale model of San Francisco Bay diligently reproduces every ebb and flow of its tidal waters. It was constructed by the Army Corps of Engineers for the purpose of scientific research.

2100 Bridgeway. Tel: (415) 332 3871; www.spn.usace.army.mil/bmvc
Open: Tue–Fri 9am–4pm, weekends 10am–5pm. Closed: Sun & Mon in winter. Free admission.

Sonoma Valley

If the Napa Valley is a young and ever-smiling hostess in a designer business suit, then the parallel Sonoma Valley likes the laid-back, smart-jeaned, mature and natural look. Its wines are just as fine, the atmosphere in the vineyards less intense, but the big difference is that Sonoma has history – and it knows it.

The town of Sonoma was founded in 1823, marking the northern end of the Mission line the Spanish started building from San Diego in 1769. Its spacious central plaza also witnessed the never-to-be-forgotten Bear Flag Revolt of 1846, which proclaimed the independent republic of California that lasted for almost a whole month.

Sonoma State Historic Park

The key buildings in the town's history are now part of the Sonoma State Historic Park. In the northeast corner of the central Plaza stands the restored Mission San Francisco Solano de Sonoma (*tel: (707) 938 9560*). Just across 1st East Street are the two-storey barracks (*tel: (707) 939 9420*), which now house a museum and Visitor Center. The Victorian home of General Vallejo, the Mexican commander overthrown by the Bear Flag revolutionaries, is a short drive west along Spain Street. (*tel: (707) 938 9559*); *www.parks.ca.gov. Open: daily 10am–5pm. Admission charge.*

72km (45 miles) north. Sonoma Valley Visitors Bureau: 453 1st St East, Sonoma. Tel: (866) 996 1090, (707) 996 1090; www.sonomavalley.com Bus: Golden Gate Transit.

Tiburon

Like Sausalito, Tiburon is a lazy, riviera-style pleasure port that oozes wellbeing. Ferry connections with San Francisco and nearby Angel Island (*see p134*) make it a popular objective for an easy-going cruise or cycling tour. There's not much to do, save browse the shops along Main Street and Ark Row and drink in the Bay views from waterfront deck cafés. *19km (12 miles) north via US 101 and Highway 131. Ferry: Blue & Gold Fleet from Pier 41 or Ferry Building. Bus: Golden Gate Transit.*

Hot-air balloon drifts above vineyards in the Napa Valley

South Bay

Filoli

Willis Polk designed this stately home in 1915 for the wealthy San Franciscan gold-mining magnate William Bowers Bourn II. The property reflects its owner's admiration for the country estates of Ireland, and is named from the first letters in his favourite motto: 'Fight for a just cause, Love your fellow man, Live a good life'. The 43-room house includes a ballroom decorated with scenes from Killarney, while the surrounding 265-hectare (654-acre) estate includes splendid mature gardens, a tearoom and gift shop.

40km (25 miles) south via Interstate 280, take Cañada Road exit. Tel: (650) 364 8300; www.filoli.org. Open: Tue–Sat, mid-Feb–late Oct, 10am–3.30pm, Sun 11am–3.30pm. Guided & self-guided tours. Admission charge.

Mount Diablo State Park

Extraordinary views over the Bay Area are the worthwhile reward for negotiating the bottleneck freeways and urban sprawl that gnaw the flanks of this 1,173-m (3,849-ft) mountain on the western edge of Central Valley. The summit is accessible by car (watch out for *kamikaze* chipmunks) but also gained with astonishing ease by local mountain-bikers. Around this lies the gentle wilderness of the park, with panoramic picnic spots, trails and campsites. The Park Office is at the junction of North Gate Road and Mount Diablo Scenic Boulevard.

Information is also available from the small museum inside the summit watchtower (*Wed–Sun 10am–4pm*).

Country-house splendour at Filoli Mansion

53km (33 miles) east via Walnut Creek. Take Diablo Rd exit off Interstate 680 at Danville. Tel: (925) 837 2525; www.parks.ca.gov. Open: 8am–dusk. Views can be hazy in summer. Admission charge for vehicles.

Palo Alto
Stanford University

Founded in 1885 by the railway baron Leland Stanford, this is one of America's top private universities with some 14,900 students and close links to the adjacent Silicon Valley. The main entrance to the 3,310-hectare (8,180-acre) campus is via Palm Drive on its north side. This leads to its charming centrepiece, the neo-Romanesque arcaded Main Quad. There is a Visitor Center here where you can pick up a map.

The University opened in 1891 and is dedicated to Stanford's son Leland Jr, who died of typhoid aged 15. The Memorial Church on the far side of the Quad is a cathedral-like shrine to the family. For an overview of the campus take the lift up the 87-m (285-ft) **Hoover Tower**, a short walk to the east.

A small museum at its base pays homage to Stanford's most famous student, the Republican President Herbert Hoover. The 1989 Loma Prieta earthquake damaged several buildings in the University, including the Stanford Museum of Art that reopened as the renamed **Cantor Center for Visual Arts** (*tel: (650) 723 4177; www.stanford.edu/dept/ccva Open: Wed–Sun 11am–5pm, Thur to 8pm. Closed: Mon & Tue. Free admission.*

*Palo Alto is 53km (33 miles) southeast on US 101. Take University Ave south past the railway station.
Stanford University: Tel: (650) 723 2560; www.stanford.edu. Information Centers open: Mon–Fri 8am–5pm, Sat–Sun 9am–5pm. Call for visitor center hours and tours. Hoover Tower Observation Platform: tel: (650) 723 2053. Open: daily during school term 10am–4.30pm (call for opening times during University holidays). Rail: CalTrain. Bus: SamTrans.*

Paramount's Great America

Scenes from the films made by Paramount Pictures provide the theme for this thrill-giving 40.5-hectare (100-acre) family entertainment park. Attractions include adventure rides inspired by *Top Gun, Survivor, The Ride,* and children's shows starring Scooby-Doo and familiar cartoon characters.
72km (45 miles) southeast on US 101, take Great America Parkway exit. 5km (3 miles) north of San Jose. Tel: (408) 988 1776; www.pgathrills.com. Open: daily Apr–Oct and irregular dates rest of the year. Park opens 10am, closing times vary. Admission charge.

Point Año Nuevo
Año Nuevo State Reserve

This coastal wildlife reserve is best known for its elephant seals, but whale watching and seabirds are other draws. The main breeding season for the 7,000 seals that gather in orgiastic heaps on Bight Beach and in the abandoned lighthouse buildings of Año Nuevo Island just offshore, is between December and March. At this time access is only by guided walk (with reservations necessary), but you can also see seals here at other times. All visitors must get a permit from the Visitor Center.
89km (55 miles) south on Highway 1 (see p126). Tel: (650) 879 0227; www.parks.ca.gov. Open: daily Apr–Aug 8.30am–3.30pm (till 3pm Sept–Nov). For advance reservation on guided walks 15 Dec–Mar tel: 800 444 4445 (toll-free), international reservations (916) 638 5883. http://anonuevo.reserveamerica.com Closed: 1–14 Dec. Admission charge for vehicle and walks.

Groves of academia: the serene campus of Stanford University, Palo Alto

San Jose

San Jose may lack the compact, great city feel of San Francisco, but the capital of Silicon Valley does have several unique sights worth catching if you're in the mood.

Rosicrucian Museum

The American headquarters of the Rosicrucian Order, whose members draw inspiration from a mystical and esoteric philosophy that flourished in ancient Egypt, can be found in serene, campus-like grounds to the west of Downtown. Papyrus groves and statues of animal deities stand outside an Egyptian Museum modelled on the Temple of Amon at Karnak. Exhibits include many artefacts from the days of the Pharaohs, including a walk-in replica of a step pyramid, and a Planetarium.

1342 Naglee Ave. Tel: (408) 947 3635; www.egyptianmuseum.org
Open: Mon–Fri 10am–5pm, weekends 11am–6pm. Admission charge.

Tech Museum of Innovation

Motivated by a desire to explain in layman's terms the wonderful but often baffling inventions that have emerged from Silicon Valley, this museum puts great faith in enlightenment through interaction. Most exhibits will be updated or new by 2007. Visitors are invited to design a product using a microchip, design a dream mountain bike, learn the inner workings of the Internet, or explore genetic engineering issues.

201 South Market St. Tel: (408) 294 8324; www.techmuseum.org. Open: Tue–Sun 10am–5pm. Closed: Mon. Admission charge.

Winchester Mystery House

In 1884, following a meeting with a Boston psychic, the tormented and reclusive daughter-in-law of the inventor of the Winchester rifle set builders to work on a neverending madhouse that would hopefully appease the spirits of people killed and injured by the company's firearms. Carpenters worked round the clock for the next 38 years until her death, creating a 160-room Addams Family-style luxury residence using the very best materials.

The result is spooky mayhem. Skylights in the floor and chimney breasts that stop short of the roof, flights of steps two-inches high,

The spirit of ancient Egypt is alive and well in the Rosicrucian Museum in San Jose

staircases that rise into the ceiling, doors leading to thin air. Sounds like a gimmick? Well, 10,000 windows, 2,000 doors, 52 skylights, 47 fireplaces, 40 staircases, six kitchens, three lifts, two bathrooms and a shower would argue differently.

525 South Winchester Blvd. Tel: (408) 247 2101; www.winchestermysteryhouse.com Open: guided tours daily 9am–5pm, open till later some weekends and summer. Admission charge.

A dazzling interior display at the Tech Museum of Innovation, San Jose

80km (50 miles) southeast on US 101. San Jose Convention & Visitors Bureau: 408 Almaden Blvd. Tel: (800) 726 5673, (408) 295 9600; www.sanjose.org Rail: CalTrain. Bus: Greyhound.

San Mateo
Coyote Point Museum for Environmental Education

Just south of San Francisco International Airport, this is an excellent waterside museum explaining the natural history of the Bay Area. Core exhibits illustrate the seven major habitats in the region, with the help of resident wildlife stars ranging from indolent rattlesnakes and banana slugs to hyper-athletic river otters. Few museums provide such a meaningful explanation of the natural world as this – while jumbo jets tear through the skies above.

1651 Coyote Point Drive. Tel: (650) 342 7755; www.coyoteptmuseum.org Open: Tue–Sat 10am–5pm, Sun noon–5pm. Closed: Mon. Admission charge (free first Wed of every month). 27km (17 miles) south on US 101. Rail: CalTrain. Bus: SamTrans.

Santa Cruz

Santa Cruz has been a classic American seaside resort since the creation of its funfair Boardwalk in 1907. With its safe, sandy beach, historic amusements and a pier jutting into Monterey Bay, the town is a good place to pause while driving Highway 1 – and a must if you have children on board.

Bobcat at the Coyote Point Museum for Environmental Education

Santa Cruz Beach Boardwalk
A jubilant 1911 Looff Carousel and a
screaming 1924 Giant Dipper wooden
roller coaster are the star attractions in
this well-organised parade of seaside
thrills. Discover the culinary mysteries
of beef jerky, salt water taffy, gyros and
funnel cakes as you tread the boards to a
Beach Boys soundtrack. The Historium
on the second floor of Neptune's
Kingdom gives a fascinating historical
account of the Boardwalk and the good
old days when crowds flocked to see
Mighty Bosco perform a 'Stratosphere
Dive' from 24m (80ft) up into water
only 2.5m (8ft) deep.
400 Beach St. Tel: (831) 423 5590;
www.beachboardwalk.com. Open:
Memorial Day (last Mon in May)–Labor
Day (first Mon in Sept), most weekends
and holidays. Admission charge for rides.

119km (74 miles) south on Highway 1
(see p126).

Silicon Valley
The southern end of San Francisco
Bay is known as Silicon Valley, which
stretches for 24km (15 miles) between
Palo Alto and its capital, San Jose.

A century ago this land was dappled
with orchards and vineyards, but since
the 1970s it has grown prosperously
urban from harvesting AppleMacs and
IBMs. Its nickname derives from the
silicon chip, a popular term for the
minuscule electronic circuits stored on a
silicon crystal that power computers and
many other technological wonders.

Encouraged by the presence of
progressive universities like Stanford and
Berkeley, hi-tech industries have gathered
in Santa Clara County since the 1950s.
Electronics and computer empires have
grown from seeds planted by young
scientists like Steve Jobs and Steve
Wozniak, who in 1975 set out to design a
powerful computer for home and office
use. They started work in Jobs' garage
with funds raised by selling a Volkswagen
van, calling their new-fangled invention
'Apple' as it represented the cleanness and
simplicity they sought. Within six years
they had 4,000 employees and a billion-
dollar turnover.

Today, after a dot-com 'bust' a few
years ago, there are still information
technology and computer firms working
in the Valley. Commentators compared
the original boom to a second gold rush
– accurate until the underpinnings gave
way somewhat with the economic
decline at the start of the new
millennium. Ironically, the new
communications and information
technologies it has spawned mean that
businesses no longer need to be located
here, and now every go-ahead nation has
its own Silicon Strip, Coast or Valley.

State historic marker in front of the house and
garage in which Silicon Valley was born with the
Hewlett-Packard Corporation in 1938

Main entrance to the Apple Computer campus in Silicon Valley, Cupertino

Tour: Wine valleys

For many visitors to San Francisco a trip to the Napa Valley, the amiable headquarters of the American wine industry, is as essential as a cable-car ride. This 241-km (150-mile) round tour, which also visits the less commercial Sonoma Valley, offers a very Californian blend of wine tasting, culture and picnics on the lawn.

Allow at least a full day, starting early.

This itinerary begins, as all great journeys should, on the Golden Gate Bridge.

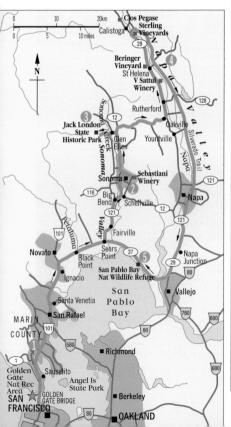

1 Marin County

Driving north, follow US 101 as it winds up through Marin County to San Rafael, the county's largest city where the Spanish founded a Mission in 1817. *13km (8 miles) further north turn right for Highway 37. Cross the Petaluma River then turn left onto Highway 121. Follow the signs into Sonoma via Highway 12, continuing to the central Plaza. Turn right by the Mission along East Spain Street to reach the Sebastiani Vineyards & Winery.*

2 Sonoma

The history of the third-generation, family-owned Sebastiani vineyard stretches back to the arrival of Samuele Sebastiani from Tuscany in 1895. A free and informative half-hour winery and tasting tour (*389 4th St East. Tel: 800 888 5532, ext 3230; www.sebastiani.com*) admits visitors into its pungent and shadowy world, where old-world know-how meets state-of-the-art technology and the barrels come as mighty as redwood trees. A short walk west along East Spain Street brings you to Sonoma's central plaza and Mission buildings (*see p116–17*).

Leave Sonoma via West Napa St, travelling north along Highway 12 (signposted to Santa Rosa). Turn left for Glen Ellen, then turn right by the Jack London Lodge for the Jack London State Historic Park.

3 Jack London State Historic Park

On the way up you will pass the charming Benziger Family Winery (*tel: (888) 490 2739; www.benziger.com*), where visitors can try the wine and follow a self-guided tour of the vineyards. Jack London State Historic Park was the final home of the roving, bestselling author Jack London (*see p114*).

Return the same way to Highway 12. Continue north, then turn right onto Trinity Rd, signposted to Oakville. This scenic drive cuts over the hills to the Napa Valley. Turn left when you reach Highway 29.

4 Napa Valley

Forming a spine for the Napa Valley, Highway 29 is lined with flagship wineries built in ostentatious styles that range from pompous châteaux to post-modernist bunkers. This tour recommends starting with a picnic under the trees at the V Sattui Winery (*tel: (707) 963 7774; www.vsattui.com*), on the right, where there is a delicatessen.

Further north in St Helena, the German-origin Beringer Vineyards (*tel: (707) 967 4412; www.beringer.com*), on the left, and its landmark 1876 Rhine House exemplify the old-money Napa winery.

Continue north towards Calistoga, but turn right just before it into Dunaweal Lane. Sterling Vineyards (*tel: (800) 726 6136; www.sterlingvineyards.com*) is on

the right, with its 1968 whitewashed pseudo-Greek hilltop monastery reached by gondola. Clos Pegase (*tel: (707) 942 4981; www.clospegase.com*), on the opposite side of the road, is the winery-as-art temple, with a 1986 show house and lawns adorned with modern sculpture.

Continue along Dunaweal Lane and turn right to join the Silverado Trail, a former stagecoach route that runs south, parallel and across the valley to Highway 29. Follow it down to Napa, joining with Highway 121, then take Highway 29 towards Vallejo. Turn right onto Highway 37.

5 San Pablo Bay

This route crosses the mouth of the Napa River to skirt the level shoreline of the San Pablo Bay National Wildlife Refuge.

Continue back to US 101, turning south for the Golden Gate Bridge and San Francisco.

Blame it all on the god of wine – sculpture at Clos Pegase Winery

Tour: Highway 1

This 257-km (160-mile) tour winds south along Highway 1, one of the most famous coastal roads in America, to visit the seaside resort of Santa Cruz. The return route climbs inland to enjoy the redwood forests and panoramas of the Santa Cruz Mountains. If you want to laze on the beach or hike in the woods, consider spending a night in or near Santa Cruz. (*For map of route, see p109.*)
Allow one or two days.

This itinerary leaves San Francisco via Daly City. Follow any sign south for Interstate 280, then take the Pacifica exit to pick up Highway 1.

1 Highway 1

The road winds south hugging the coast, passing the fragrant eucalyptus woods of

The crescent of sand named Half Moon Bay

the **San Pedro Valley Park** and beaches and headlands that in summer can be eerily shrouded in fog. Half Moon Bay has a splendid crescent of sands, and is famous for its October Pumpkin Festival, when the surrounding fields turn bright orange. Many of the towns along here were originally settled by Portuguese and Italian farmers and fishermen. A noticeable landmark is the 1872 34-m (115-ft) **Pigeon Point Lighthouse** (*tel: (650) 879 2120; www.parks.ca.gov,* guided tours of grounds only on Fri–Sun 10am–4pm). A youth hostel (*tel: (650) 879 0633*) occupies its outbuildings.
Turn right for Año Nuevo State Reserve.

2 Point Año Nuevo

Whale-watching and observing breeding elephant seals are the main attractions at this wildlife sanctuary (*see pp119*).
Continue southeast along Highway 1.

3 Santa Cruz

The road sweeps down past the fog-less blue Pacific to this thoroughly American seaside resort. Turn right into Bay Street, following signs to the Beach

Boardwalk (*see p122*).
*When you leave Santa Cruz, cross
Highway 1 to drive north up Highway 9.*

4 Big Basin Redwoods State Park
The road snakes up into the shady
woods and inland villages that border
the River San Lorenzo. Continue
climbing through the Henry Cowell
Redwoods State Park to Ben Lomond
and then Boulder Creek, where you
might want to stop for a snack or to buy
some picnic provisions. Turn left up
Highway 236, passing a golf course to
reach the Big Basin Redwoods State Park
(*tel: (831) 331 8860; www.parks.ca.gov*).
(If you prefer to omit this detour,
continue along Highway 9.)

With 7,689 hectares (19,000 acres) of
redwood forest and parkland, Big Basin
is a perfect place to fall in love with trees
that were mere striplings when
Columbus discovered the New World.
An hour-long trail guides visitors round
some of its mightiest examples,
including the 100-m (329-ft) tall
'Mother' and the 2,000-year-old 'Father'
of the forest.
*Continue driving north through the park
on Highway 236. This descends to rejoin
Highway 9. Turn left following the sign for
Saratoga. When you reach Skyline
Boulevard (Highway 35) turn left,
signposted to San Francisco.*

5 Skyline Boulevard
This beautiful drive meanders north
through the forests and parks of the
Santa Cruz Mountains, offering
alternating views west to the sea and
east to the South Bay. Lonely rows of
mailboxes are the only signs of life –
spare time to stop at a vista point and
enjoy the tranquillity.
*Turn right down Highway 84, signposted
to Woodside, to join the Junípero Serra
Freeway (Interstate 280). Continue north
to San Francisco.*

Big trees at Big Basin – one of the best spots in the Bay Area to enjoy the majesty of redwood forests

Getting away from it all

Everyone knows that green hills, sandy beaches and outdoor adventures are just a short drive or ferry ride away from San Francisco. What's remarkable is that they can all be found within the city too.

Savouring the view from Twin Peaks

Ballooning

Balloons Above the Valley
Early-morning flights over Napa Valley.
603 California Blvd, Napa.
Tel: (800) 464 6824, (707) 253 2222;
www.balloonsabovethevalley.com

A Balloon Over Sonoma
Flights over Sonoma Valley from winery sites.
Tel: (707) 546 3360;
www.aballoonoversonoma.com

Cycling

The mountain bike was invented on the slopes of Mount Tamalpais, and San Francisco has much to offer the cyclist who doesn't mind the odd climb.

You could follow part of the 49-Mile Scenic Drive (*see pp104–5*), and on Sundays, when John F Kennedy Drive is closed, Golden Gate Park offers 12km (7¹/₂ miles) of cycling.

Take a ride across Golden Gate Bridge (*see p102*). Bicycles can be taken on ferries and BART – rental shops can suggest routes. Ring first to check availability and what deposit is required.

Bay City Bike
2661 Taylor St (near Fisherman's Wharf).
Tel: (415) 346 2453; www.baycitybike.com
Golden Gate Park Skate & Bike
3038 Fulton St. Tel: (416) 668 1117.

Hiking

There is a rich choice of trails in and around San Francisco. The Marin Headlands, Mount Tamalpais, Angel Island and all parts of the Golden Gate National Recreation Area are popular tramping grounds (*see individual entries*).

Visitor Centers can provide routes and maps, and bookstores sell specialist guides.

Horse riding

See p153.

Scenic flights

Taking to the skies is an unbeatable way to see the city and the Bay; most companies provide a door-to-door service.

San Francisco Seaplane Tours
Seaplane flights over the Bay and city from Pier 39 or Sausalito.
Tel: (888) 732 7526, (415) 332 4843;
www.seaplane.com
San Francisco Helicopter Tours
Helicopter flights over the city, Bay and Wine Country.
Tel: (800) 400 2404, (650) 635 4500;
www.sfhelicoptertours.com
San Francisco Hang Gliding
Tandem hang glider flights from Mt

Tamalpais over the redwoods to Stinson Beach.
Tel: (408) 262 7189;
www.sfhanggliding.com

Whale watching
Oceanic Society Expeditions
High season is December to April, when grey whales migrating between Alaska and Mexico pass by.
Fort Mason Center, Building E.
Tel: (415) 474 3385;
www.oceanicsociety.org
Bay Adventures
Local whale watching and day trips to the Farallon Islands.
Tel: (415) 331 0444;
www.sfbayadventures.com

Beaches
San Francisco lacks the beaches and seaside culture of southern California, but there are still plenty of sands and rolling Pacific waves to enjoy in the city and nearby.

Baker Beach
On the southwest side of the Presidio, this is the most popular beach in city limits. The sea is cold and unsafe for swimming, but its sands are enjoyed by walkers and sunbathers – nude at the northern end.
Take Bowley St then Gibson Rd west from Lincoln Blvd. Bus: 29.
China Beach
This small pocket of sand in the Seacliff district gets its name from the Chinese fishing junks that once anchored here. Swimming is safe, with lifeguards on duty in the summer.
North of Seacliff Ave. Bus: 29.

Drake's Beach
See p135.
Ocean Beach
Kite-fliers, jilted lovers, joggers, film-makers, fog addicts, surf heroes – Ocean Beach, with four miles of wind-ravaged sands running down the west side of the city from the Cliff House to Fort Funston, will please anyone except swimmers, as the strong currents make bathing unsafe.
By Great Highway. Metro: L & N. Bus: 5, 16AX, 18, 31, 48, 71.

Waiting for a wave at Fort Point – San Francisco's waters are often cold and rough

Stinson Beach

Complement a visit to Muir Woods or Mount Tamalpais State Park (*see p115 & p134*) with a laze on the Bay Area's best beach – a 5.5-km (3¹/₂-mile) sandbar where swimming is safe and sheltered. There are picnic facilities, lifeguards in summer and plenty of people to watch.

32km (20 miles) northwest via Highway 1. Tel: (415) 868 1922. www.stinsonbeachonline.com, www.nps.gov/muwo/stbe. Open: daily 9am–sunset. Parking charge. Traffic can be slow on summer weekends. Bus: Golden Gate Transit at weekends.

Boat trips

You won't have 'done' San Francisco till you've had a spin on the Bay. Services are geared to suit both commuters and

A trip across the Bay is an essential part of any visit to San Francisco – and great fun

visitors, and depart from either Fisherman's Wharf or the Ferry Building. Call to check times.

Blue & Gold Fleet

Regular ferry services to Oakland, Alameda, Sausalito, Tiburon, Vallejo. Excursions: Bay cruises, Alcatraz, Angel Island.

Tel: (415)705 5555; www.blueandgoldfleet.com

Golden Gate Ferries

Regular ferry services to Sausalito and Larkspur departing from the Ferry Building.

Ferry Building, The Embarcadero and Market St. Tel: (415) 455 2000, 511 (toll-free); www.goldengate.org

Red and White Fleet

Bay cruises.

Departures from Pier 413/2. Tel: (415) 673 2900; www.redandwhite.com

City parks

Don't think Golden Gate Park and the Presidio (*see p62 & p87*) are the only green spaces in San Francisco.

Aquatic Park

See p36.

Crissy Field

On the northern shore of the Presidio, Crissy Field was established as a military airfield in 1919 and played a pioneering role in early American aviation. A refurbished part of the Golden Gate National Recreation Area, it is a peaceful, often windy, open space. The adjacent waters are popular with experienced windsurfers.

Mason St. Bus: 29.

Lake Merced

In the southwest corner of the city, this tranquil natural lake is mainly used for boating, trout fishing and relaxation in the scenic parkland that surounds it.

By Lake Merced Blvd. Bus: 18.

Lincoln Park

A green frame for the California Palace of the Legion of Honor (*see p38*), Lincoln Park used to be the site of San Francisco's municipal cemetery before this was re-sited in 1909 to the south of the city at Colma in San Mateo County. The 109-hectare (270-acre) area was landscaped by John McLaren, the designer of Golden Gate Park, and today incorporates an 18-hole public golf course and several walking trails.

Main entrance at Clement St & 34th Ave. Bus: 18 & 38.

Marina Green

This strip of green between Fort Mason and the Presidio stages a free daily display of the self-punishing sports and fitness regimes that are apparently crucial to the survival of many San Franciscans. You may think you've stumbled on a city marathon, but in fact it's just the regular tide of after-work, iPod-carrying joggers pounding the shoreline.

This area was developed for the 1915 Panama-Pacific International Exposition, and now has a marina and the private St Francis Yacht Club.

At the far eastern end of the adjacent West Harbor Jetty is a Wave Organ developed by workers from the Exploratorium, with some 20 pipes playing liquid music.

By Marina Blvd. Bus: 22 & 30.

Lake Merced – a park for fishing and dreaming

Sigmund Stern Memorial Grove

A 25.5 hectare (63-acre) wooded park in the sedate southwest of the city, worth visiting for the free concerts staged in its natural amphitheatre on Sunday afternoons in the summer.

By 19th Ave & Sloat Blvd.
Tel: (415) 252 6252; www.sterngrove.org
Metro: M. Bus: 23 & 28.

Sutro Heights Park

Overlooking the north end of Ocean Beach, this park was originally the mansion and enthusiastically nurtured grounds of the property magnate Adolph Sutro. After his family left in 1938 the house fell into ruins and was eventually demolished. Since 1976 its gardens have been part of the Golden Gate National Recreation Area – now a strange and forgotten, often fog-bound, cliff-top sanctuary.

At the west end of Point Lobos Ave.
Bus: 18, 38, 38L.

Golden Gate National Recreation Park

Many of the green splashes on the San Francisco map belong to the 30,512-hectare (75,398-acre) Golden Gate National Recreation Area (GGNRA), the most visited national park in the United States. Established in 1972, its protected lands and waters stretch south from Point Reyes Station to Sweeney Ridge, and include historic attractions such as Alcatraz, the Presidio and the San Francisco Maritime National Historic Park. Most of the city's northern and western shoreline falls under its jurisdiction, including Fort Mason, Crissy Field, Ocean Beach and Fort Funston. North of the Golden Gate Bridge, the GGNRA's realm includes the Marin Headlands, Muir Woods and Stinson Beach.

To get the best of GGNRA, buy a copy of the official *Park Guide* that includes maps and trail information. Free or inexpensive literature with information on walks, biking and horse riding trails, wildlife, recreational facilities and picnic spots is also available from Visitor Centers at main sites. A free quarterly calendar of what's on, *Park News*, available online, lists the detailed programme of events in the park, which vary from a backcountry mountain-bike ride to a peek around the Presidio Cemetery. Information is also available from GGNRA Park Headquarters, Building 201, Fort Mason Center *tel: (415) 561 4700; www.nps.gov.goga*

Golden Gate Promenade

This 6.5-km (4-mile) walk runs along San Francisco's northern shoreline from Aquatic Park to Fort Point, offering fine views of Golden Gate Bridge and plenty of stress-defusing sea air.

Fort Funston

Named after General Frederick Funston, the military commander of the Presidio at the time of the 1906 earthquake, these windy cliffs and dunes to the south of Ocean Beach are popular with hikers, horse riders and hang gliders.
Tel: (415) 561 4323;
www.nps.gov/goga/fofu
Bus: 88 (check schedule and route).

Land's End

At the northern edge of Lincoln Park, these wild, shipwrecking headlands can be reached by a coastal trail running between the California Palace of the Legion of Honor and Point Lobos.
Bus: 18.

Olema Valley

Running north–south alongside Bolinas Ridge for nine miles, this pastoral Marin County valley, part of Point Reyes National Seashore, makes a pleasant drive past sweeping fields, historic farms and orchards.
48km (30 miles) north on Highway 1.
Bear Valley Visitor Center:
Tel: (415) 464 5100;
www.nps.gov/muwo/olva

Sweeney Ridge

The mountain ridge from which San Francisco Bay was first seen by European eyes is now the focal point of a 424-hectare (1,047-acre) nature park to the south of San Francisco. The Spanish Captain Gaspar de Portolá climbed up here on 4 November, 1769 during a 10-month expedition, searching for Monterey Bay. The 8-km (5-mile) return Sweeney Ridge Trail leads up to the Portola Discovery Site, but be aware that fog can often obscure this historic view. There are several trails to follow through scrub and grassland, and on a good day you can see the Farallon Islands, Point Reyes and Mount Diablo.

21km (13 miles) south, near San Bruno. Take Sneath Lane exit from Highway 35 (Skyline Blvd) or Interstate 280. Tel: (415) 561 4700; www.nps.gov/goga/clho/swri

Redwood palaces
The tallest trees in the world, coastal redwoods thrive in the cool, moist environment of the fog belts of California and Oregon. *Sequoia sempervirens* can often grow to heights of over 91m (300ft), though it is their inland relatives *Sequoia gigantea*, the giant sequoias on the western slopes of the Sierra Nevada mountains, that have the longer lifespan and greater bulk. The trees' red bark is resistant to fire, fungus and insects, and their thick, shallow roots extend up to 30.5m (100ft) to catch water condensed from the fog passing through the branches above. Walk amidst them at Muir Woods (*see p115*).

Visitors enjoying the Golden Gate Promenade along San Francisco Bay, looking toward the Golden Gate Bridge, part of the Golden Gate National Recreation Area

The cycling map in the state park on Angel Island is an excellent guide

Islands
Angel Island State Park
Now a peaceful state park that looms over the bustle of the Bay, 299-hectare (740-acre) Angel Island was once the Pacific equivalent of New York's Ellis Island. From 1910 to 1940 an immigration station here processed refugees and would-be settlers from Asia and elsewhere, including around 175,000 Chinese. Remnants of this and military garrisons built in the second half of the 19th century survive on the island.

Angel Island is the largest island in the Bay and has a Visitor Center, picnic sites, tram tours and 19km (12 miles) of roads and hiking trails winding up to its 237-m (776-ft) summit, Mount

Livermore. Take a bicycle, or rent a kayak, picnic and have a lazy day.
Park Information: tel: (415) 435 1915; www.parks.ca.gov
Ferry: Blue & Gold Fleet from Pier 41, San Francisco; Angel Island Ferry from Tiburon (tel: (415) 435 2131; http://angelislandferry.com).

Farallon Islands
A cluster of small granite islands 48km (30 miles) west of San Francisco – off-limits to visitors – the Farallons are a rocky wildlife sanctuary inhabited by seals, sea lions and a host of seabirds including puffins, cormorants, guillemots and some 25,000 gulls. **Oceanic Society Expeditions** arrange escorted whale-, dolphin- and bird-watching trips.
Tel: (415) 474 3385; www.oceanicsociety.org

Mount Tamalpais State Park
If you like hiking, Mount Tam is the perfect host. Rising to 784m (2,571ft), it has over 322km (200 miles) of trails to suit all abilities and vista requirements – including one from Panoramic Highway down to Muir Woods and a path following what used to be the world's crookedest railway line. The park covers 2,550 hectares (6,300 acres), picnic and camping sites and a Mountain Theater. Information can be picked up at the Pantoll Ranger Station on Panoramic Highway. Access to the summit may be restricted if there is a fire hazard.
24km (15 miles) north via Highway 1 and Panoramic Highway. Tel: (415) 388 2070; www.parks.ca.gov

Point Reyes National Seashore

For a sense of the natural peace, space and bounty that must have filled the hearts of the first Europeans to visit the Bay Area, head for this 67,000-acre protected coastline. Information is available from the Bear Valley Visitor Center, a short drive west of Olema. Point Reyes National Seashore lies on the west side of the San Andreas Fault – an Earthquake Trail in the park calmly explains that you are standing in a rift between the Pacific and North American tectonic plates.

One rewarding goal here is **Drake's Beach**, a windswept beach 24km (15 miles) west of the Visitor Center. This is thought to be the site where the English seafarer Sir Francis Drake landed on 17 June, 1579 to claim 'Nova Albion' (New England) for his queen, Elizabeth I. He and his crew stayed here for five weeks, trading with the native Miwok Indians and victualling the *Golden Hind* before continuing their circumnavigation of the globe. British visitors will reflect, as Drake surely did, on how similar this coastal landscape is to that of their homeland.

Much of the coast here is home to isolated ranches dating back to the mid-19th century. Connoisseurs of land's ends will press on to Point Reyes Lighthouse, a favourite spot for whale watching, reached by a long and winding road and a 308-step descent. In winter, a shuttle bus (fee charged) saves congestion for visitors arriving to watch for grey whales and elephant seals. San Francisco may be less than one-and-a-half hour's drive away, but here you feel truly away from it all.

56km (35 miles) northwest via US 101 and Sir Francis Drake Blvd.
Visitor Center: Tel: (415) 464 5100; www.nps.gov/pore. Free access.

Looking south across San Francisco Bay towards the city of San Francisco from the top of Mount Tamalpais, Mount Tamalpais State Park

Curious elephant seals at Point Año Nuevo

Wildlife

Nature is never far away in San Francisco. You'll find buffalo roaming in Golden Gate Park, sea lions sunbathing on pontoons beside Pier 39, brown pelicans posing beside Cliff House – there's even a small community of Californian salamanders living on the parade ground at Alcatraz. The Bay Area provides ready access to a great variety of wildlife habitats around the Bay, with informative leaflets and free guided tours with rangers available in most parts of the Golden Gate National Recreation Area.

The Pacific Ocean is a prime cause of local addiction to binoculars. Blue, humpback, killer and grey whales all pass by offshore in their migration along the length of America's West Coast. Every year some 15,000 grey whales make a round trip between summer feeding grounds in the Bering Straits and winter breeding grounds off Mexico, travelling over 16,000km (10,000 miles) in less than two months. December to April is the best time to watch them.

California sea lions, the larger Steller sea lions, harbour seals and enormous elephant seals all benefit from protected marine life sanctuaries such as the Farallon Islands, Point Reyes National Seashore and Point Año Nuevo. Seabirds are also thriving from the environmental awareness of today's Bay Area residents

– egg-hunters in the gold rush virtually wiped out the gull colonies on Alcatraz, but today nests of breeding birds are an unexpected treat for visitors to the island in June.

Inland, California's famous redwood forests offer much more than magnificent trees. Black-tailed deer, raccoons, grey squirrels and chipmunks are some residents, while birdlife ranges from the beautiful blue-black Steller's jay to obscure characters with hip-hop names like towhee, junco and vireo. Hawk-lovers should head for the Marin Headlands between September and October, when at peak times over 2,000 birds a day can be seen migrating south.

Golden Gate Raptor Observatory.
Tel: (415) 331 0730; www.ggro.org

The seemingly unwieldy pelican (top) and cormorants gathering at Point Lobos (above)

Shopping

Whilst most of us shop to live, many Californians seem to live to shop. Best seen as a source of public therapy, San Francisco's malls and shopping streets are full of lovely things to wander amongst, admire and maybe even buy.

Sports gear supporting the city's baseball and football teams is a popular buy

Where to shop

San Francisco's shopping heart is Union Square and its neighbouring blocks. Here you will find department stores such as Macy's and Neiman Marcus, and designer shops like Emporio Armani, Tiffany and Saks Fifth Avenue. Fisherman's Wharf and Chinatown have everything a tourist needs (and plenty you don't), but the most rewarding shopping will probably result from casual finds made while visiting neighbourhoods such as North Beach, Union Street, Hayes Valley and the Haight-Ashbury. These areas all have small shops with individual style. If you need to take presents home, museum stores, like those at SFMOMA, The Museum of Craft and Folk Art, and the California Academy of Sciences, are a good source.

Opening hours

Most shops are open at least Monday to Saturday 10am–6pm, with extended hours some evenings and Sunday opening depending on their location and merchandise.

Prices

All purchases except unprocessed food and prescription drugs are subject to 8.5 per cent sales tax in San Francisco, unless goods are shipped outside the state (duty will be payable at their destination). As prices are displayed pre-tax, this invariably results in checks (bills) coming to odd amounts. Credit cards are widely accepted, as are dollar travellers' cheques in lieu of cash. Most retailers can provide information on packaging and shipping items home.

What to buy

Being one of the most Europhile cities in the US, San Francisco's shops are stocked with many items similar to those on sale in Europe, particularly kitchenware, stationery, youth fashion, and furniture and crafts imports from India and other Asian countries.

Good San Franciscan buys include books, particularly as so many quality authors have written about the city (*see pp16–17*), recorded music, casual wear and decorative goods for the home. Many visitors like the idea of buying a pair of Levi's jeans in the city that gave them to the world, while others go for the hippy culture posters, jewellery and tie-dye shirts on sale in Haight Street. If you find yourself with more than will go into your suitcase, Chinatown is a convenient source of inexpensive luggage.

Markets

Heart of the City Farmers' Market

Fresh fruit and vegetables from the Bay Area.
United Nations Plaza, Civic Center. Wed & Sun.

Ferry Building Farmers' Market

Fruit, vegetables, flowers and cookery demonstrations.
By the Ferry Building, The Embarcadero. Sat & Tue year-round, Thur & Sun seasonally.

Shopping centres

Anchorage Square

Souvenir shops, restaurants and street entertainers in the heart of Fisherman's Wharf.
*2800 Leavenworth St at Jefferson St.
Tel: (415) 775 6000;
www.anchoratthewharf.com*

Crocker Galleria

Glass-domed arcade with boutique shops.
*Financial District, entrances on Post and Sutter Sts, between Montgomery and Kearny Sts. Tel: (415) 393 1505;
www.shopatgalleria.com
(Also see pp98–9.)*

Embarcadero Center

Vast office and retail complex linked by above-street walkways incorporating the Hyatt Regency San Francisco Hotel.
*West of the Embarcadero between Clay and Sansome Sts.
Tel: (415) 772 0700,
www.embarcaderocenter.com /ec/*

Rincon Center

Aesthetic shopping venue centred around an art deco post office with murals by the Russian-born Anton Refregier.
*101 Spear St at Mission St.
Tel: (415) 777 4100.*

Westfield San Francisco Centre

Over 135 shops on nine floors, worth a visit just for a ride on its unique spiral escalators. Bloomingdale's debuts under a former landmark – the Emporium dome – in 2006.
*Market St at Fifth St.
Tel: (415) 512 6776;
www.westfield.com/ sanfrancisco*

Typical San Francisco souvenirs: miniature cable cars, bridges and Victorian houses

Americana
Disney Store
All your favourite cartoon characters in infinitely purchasable forms.
400 Post St, Union Square.
Tel: (415) 391 6866.
Levi's San Francisco
Union Square's home to the original jeans.
300 Post St at Stockton St.
Tel: (415) 501 0100;
www.levisstore.com
Positively Haight Street
Hippy memorabilia, rock music and T-shirts.
1400 Haight St.
Tel: (415) 252 8747.

Antiques
Jackson Square is the centre of San Francisco's antiques trade. A good eye is useful (*see p71*).

Books
Book Passage
The Bay Area's best-known independent bookseller with daily/nightly author readings and events.
Ferry Building, # 46.
Tel: (415) 835 1020;
www.bookpassage.com
Borders
Vast books and music store with café, open to 10pm weekdays.
400 Post St.
Tel: (415) 399 1633;
www.bordersstores.com

Maritime Store
Books on San Francisco and maritime subjects.
Hyde Street Pier, Fisherman's Wharf.
Tel: (415) 775 2665;
www.maritime.org

Children
Ambassador Toys
This sophisticated store has fine-quality children's books, dolls, life-sized stuffed animals, and games from around the world.
Two Embarcadero Center.
Tel: (415) 345 8697.
186 West Portal Ave.
Tel: (415) 759 8697;
www.ambassadortoys.com
Basic Brown Bear Factory
Everything you need to stuff, sew, bath, groom and dress your teddy.
The Cannery at Del Monte Square, 2801 Leavenworth St.
Tel: (866) 522 2327;
www.basicbrownbear.com
GapKids and babyGap
Practical street gear for junior and infant.
100 Post St. Tel: (415) 989 1266; www.gap.com

Clothes
Brooks Brothers
Suits and casual wear for stylish businessmen.
150 Post St at Kearney St.

Tel: (415) 397 4500;
www.brooksbrothers.com
kweejiboo clothing co.
Vintage-looking, new clothing styles for men.
1580 Haight St.
Tel: (415) 552 3555.
Hats on Post
Ladies' hats for all moods.
210 Post St, Suite 606.
Tel: (415) 392 3737.
Old Navy
Pseudo-hip clothing for the want-to-be young.
801 Market St at 4th St.
Tel: (415) 344 0375;
www.oldnavy.com

Crafts
Genji Antiques
Japanese antiques, furniture and crafts.
Japan Center, 1675 Post St. Tel: (415) 931 1616.
Gump's
Fine china, glass, jewellery and Asian antiques.
135 Post St. Tel: (415) 982 1616; www.gumps.com

Department stores
Macy's
The world in a store, spread over two buildings.
Stockton and O'Farrell Sts, Union Square.
Tel: (415) 397 3333;
www.macys.com
Neiman Marcus
Up-market clothes, jewellery and household

goods, plus the top-floor Rotunda restaurant.
150 Stockton St,
Union Square.
Tel: (415) 362 3900;
www.neimanmarcus.com

Fabric
Britex Fabrics
Four floors of dress and furnishing fabrics.
146 Geary St.
Tel: (415) 392 2910;
www.britexfabrics.com

Factory outlets
Burlington Coat Factory
Most discount ware-houses lie south of Market Street and sell clothes and sportswear for women and children. Some dedication is required to track down individual outlets, but this shopping centre conveniently gathers many bargain goods.
899 Howard St, SOMA.
Tel: (415) 495 7234;
www.burlingtoncoat
factory.com

Food and drink
Caffè Roma Coffee Roasting Co
Aromatic North Beach café and roasting house with coffee beans and blends for sale.
526 Columbus Ave. (North Beach); 885 Bryant St at
7th St (SOMA).
Tel: (415) 296 7662;
www.cafferoma.com
Il Fornaio Bakery
Superlative Italian breads and biscuits.
Levi's Plaza, 1265 Battery St. Tel: (415) 986 1100;
www.ilfornaio.com
Napa Valley Winery Exchange
Downtown Californian wine specialists.
415 Taylor St.
Tel: (415) 771 2887, (800) 653 9463; www.nvwe.com
Ten Ren Tea Co
A tempting variety of Chinese teas and herbs.
949 Grant Ave.
Tel: (415) 362 0656;
www.tenren.com

For the home
Pottery Barn
Designer crockery, cutlery and household treats.
2390 Market St.
Tel: (415) 861 0800;
2100 Chestnut St.
Tel: (415) 441 1787.
www.potterybarn.com
The Wok Shop
Everything you need to be a *dim-sum* wizard back home.
718 Grant Ave.
Tel: (415) 989 3797;
www.wokshop.com
Williams-Sonoma
Kitchenware shop with gourmet gifts and goodies.
340 Post St, Union Square.
Tel: (415) 362 9450;
www.williams-sonoma.com

Music
Amoeba Music
Live music concerts and musicians support a huge inventory of recordings – even vinyl LPs, 45s and 78s – at the San Francisco location of the largest, and arguably funkiest, indie record store in the country.
1855 Haight St.
Tel: (415) 831 1200;
www.amoebamusic.com

Tower Records
Music emporium with classical offerings by Columbus Avenue, open daily.
2525 Jones St.
Tel: (415) 441 4880;
www.towerrecords.com

Gourmet chefs shop at Williams-Sonoma

Comedians grab the stage at Cobb's Comedy Club

Entertainment

From the gold-rush days of saloons, whorehouses and gambling dens, to the hi-tech concert halls and hip dance clubs of today, San Francisco has always been a good-time city.

What's on

San Francisco's daily newspaper, *The Chronicle* (*www.sfgate.com/eguide/*), carries listings of mainstream cultural events in the city. A pink-colour bumper compendium called *Datebook* comes out on Sundays. The free *Arts Monthly* (*www.sfarts.org*) is a calendar of visual and performing arts events. The *Bay Guardian* (*www.sfbg.com*) and *SF Weekly* (*www.sfweekly.com*), both free weekly papers, are the best source for alternative entertainment and nightlife.

Events Line

24-hour recorded information compiled by the San Francisco Convention and Visitors Bureau.
Tel: (415) 391 2001.

Tickets

Tickets.com

Tickets.com has telephone and online services. A service fee is levied on each ticket.
Information and credit card bookings tel: (800) 225 2277; www.tickets.com

Mr Ticket

Best seats for top arts and sports events at prices above face value.
2065 Van Ness Ave.
Tel: (800) 424 7328, (415) 775 3031;
www.mrticket.com

TIX Bay Area

Half-price tickets for performances that day of selected theatre, dance and music events are available to personal callers. Payment in cash or travellers' cheques only for half-price tickets. Advance bookings by credit card.
Union Square on the Powell St side.
Tel: (415) 433 7827.
www.theatrebayarea.org/tix/. Open: Tue–Sat 11am–6pm (till 7pm Fri & Sat), Sun 10am–3pm. Closed: Mon.

Ballet

The world-class San Francisco Ballet company stages a regular season at the War Memorial Opera House in the Civic Center between February and May, including a production of *The Nutcracker* every Christmas.
301 Van Ness Ave. Tel: (415) 865 2000;
www.sfballet.com

Cinemas

San Franciscans are fond of film festivals – the San Francisco International Film Festival (*www.sffs.org*) in April/May is the oldest in the United States, while the San Francisco International LGBT Festival (*www.frameline.org*), screened every June, is the largest of its kind.

Ratings: G General; PG Parental Guidance advised; PG-13 some material unsuitable for children under 13; R Restricted, children under 17 need an adult companion; NC-17 no viewers under 17 admitted.

Castro
1922 movie palace with ascending Wurlitzer organ.
429 Castro St. Tel: (415) 621 6120; www.thecastrotheatre.com
Loews Theatres Metreon
The biggest multi-screen complex in town, plus IMAX, showing all the newest releases.
Metreon Center, 101 4th St at Mission St. Tel: (415) 369 6201; www.metreon.com
Red Vic
Cult hits and forgotten classics in the laid-back Haight.
1727 Haight St. Tel: (415) 668 3994; www.redvicmoviehouse.com
Sundance Kabuki
Eight screens showing indie films.
Japan Center, Post and Fillmore sts. Tel: (415) 922 4262.

Comedy and cabaret
Beach Blanket Babylon
Snow White seeks fame, fortune and true love in song and skits taken from today's newspaper headlines.
Club Fugazi, 678 Green St, North Beach. Tel: (415) 421 4222; www.beachblanketbabylon.com
Bimbo's 365 Club
Historic North Beach club with the latest bands.
1025 Columbus Ave at Chestnut St. Tel: (415) 474 0365; www.bimbos365club.com
Cobb's Comedy Club
Alternative comics – doing stand-up –

brilliant, excruciating, but always entertaining.
915 Columbus Ave. Tel: (415) 928 4320; www.cobbscomedyclub.com
Great American Music Hall
Ornate 1907 venue with live music, comics and food.
859 O'Farrell St. Tel: (415) 885 0750; www.musichallsf.com

Dance venues
Modern, classical and ethnic dance companies frequently perform at mixed-event venues around the city. See local press for who is in town.

Cowell Theater
Pier 2, Fort Mason Center. Tel: (415) 345 7575.
ODC San Francisco
3153 17th St. Tel: (415) 863 9834; www.odcdance.org
Palace of Fine Arts
330 Lyon St at Bay St. Tel: (415) 567 6642; www.palaceoffinearts.org
Theater Artaud
450 Florida St. Tel: (415) 626 4370; www.artaud.org

Give swing dance a try!

Concerts and classical music

Audium

An only-in-California theatre of sound-sculptured space.
*1616 Bush St. Tel: (415) 771 1616;
www.audium.org Open: Fri & Sat
8.30pm.*

Center for the Arts Theater

Contemporary music performances.
*701 Mission St at 3rd St, SOMA.
Tel: (415) 978 2787;
www.ybca.org/b-ybca.html*

Golden Gate Park Band

Sunday-afternoon concerts in the Music
Concourse in Golden Gate Park should
resume in late 2006.
*Between California Academy of Sciences
site and MH de Young Memorial Museum.
www.goldengateconcourse.org*

Grace Cathedral

A regular venue for concerts and choral
performances (*see p66*).

Old First Concerts

Year-round public concerts in the Old
First Presbyterian Church, from jazz to
chamber to folk to choral.
*1751 Sacramento St between Polk St &
Van Ness Ave. Tel: (415) 474 1608;
www.oldfirstconcerts.org*

San Francisco Symphony

This renowned orchestra, under music
director Michael Tilson Thomas, plays
a regular season at the Louise M Davies
Symphony Hall (Sept–early June).
*Civic Center, Van Ness Ave & Grove St.
Tel: (415) 864 6000; www.sfsymphony.org*

Nightclubs and live music

Biscuits and Blues

San Francisco's top dinner and blues club.
*401 Mason St. Tel: (415) 292 2583.
www.biscuitsandblues.com*

Nightclub on Broadway, North Beach

Empire Plush Room

Headliners and celebrities vie to appear
at this former 1920s speakeasy.
*940 Sutter St. Tel: (866) 468 3399;
www.plushroom.com*

Fillmore Auditorium

Legendary rock venue rocks on.
*1805 Geary Blvd. Tel: (415) 346 6000;
www.thefillmore.com*

Harry Denton's Starlight Room

Trendy supper club atop the Sir Francis
Drake Hotel near Union Square.
*450 Powell St. Tel: (415) 395 8595.
www.harrydenton.com*

Hornblower Dining Yachts

Dine and dance as you cruise the Bay.
*Pier 33, The Embarcadero.
Tel: (888) 467 6256. www.hornblower.com*

Jazz at Pearl's

Dining, tapas and jazz are on the menu
in this 1930s-style North Beach club.
*256 Columbus Ave. Tel: (415) 291 8255;
www.jazzatpearls.com*

Lou's Pier 47 Club

Jazz, blues and funky sounds day and
night on Fisherman's Wharf.
*300 Jefferson St. Tel: (415) 771 5687;
www.louspier47.com*

Mexican Bus
Club-hopping by bus to Caribbean and
Latin rhythms Friday and Saturday night.
Tel: (415) 546 3747;
www.mexicanbus.com
Three Babes and a Bus
Get on board the party bus for a
nightclub tour without queues.
Sat night.
Tel: 800 414 0158; www.threebabes.com
Slim's
Top bands, dancing and food in SOMA.
333 11th St. Tel: (415) 255 0333;
www.slims-sf.com

Opera
The prestigious San Francisco Opera
attracts top-name performers for its
regular season (September–December)
and June summer season at the War
Memorial Opera House.
Civic Center, Van Ness Ave & Grove St.
Tel: (415) 864 3330; www.sfopera.com

Theatre
American Conservatory Theater
Classic and contemporary repertory
drama. Season runs September to June.
Geary Theater, 415 Geary St.
Tel: (415) 749 2228; www.act-sf.org
Asian-American Theater Company
New plays, sketches and workshop
productions.
690 5th St, Suite 211. Tel: (415) 543 5738;
www.asianamericantheater.org
Curran Theatre
Broadway musicals and stage hits.
445 Geary St. Tel: (415) 551 2000;
www.bestofbroadway-sf.com
Club Fugazi
Beach Blanket Babylon – a long-running
revue with topical gags, joke costumes

and celebrity spoofs, staged in a former
1912 North Beach community hall.
678 Green St.
Tel: (415) 421 4222;
www.beachblanketbabylon.com
Golden Gate Theatre
Musicals and stage hits.
1 Taylor St.
Tel: (415) 551 2000;
www.bestofbroadway-sf.com
Magic Theater
New plays and new writers. Season runs
October to July.
Fort Mason Center, Building D.
Tel: (415) 441 8822;
www.magictheater.org
Orpheum Theatre
Broadway shows glitter in this 1926
cathedral-style venue.
Hyde and Market Sts at 8th St.
Tel: (415) 551 2000;
www.bestofbroadway-sf.com
Teatro ZinZanni
Circus and cabaret served with a five-
course dinner.
*Pier 29, The Embarcadero and Battery
Sts. Tel: (415) 438 2668;*
www.zinzanni.org

Free speech
San Franciscans' long-running love affair
with books, coffee and self-expression is
borne out by the many Spoken Word events
held around the city. Most are free and take
place in the evening – museums stage
lectures, bookstores arrange readings by
poets and writers, but the most intriguing
events are the 'open mike' evenings held in
coffee bars. Anyone can sign up to read
from their literary masterpiece, so expect to
hear anything from a moving love poem to a
transvestite's tale about trapped spiders or a
student's favourite cake recipe.

Starring San Francisco

San Francisco is only 623km (387 miles) north of Hollywood, the Los Angeles suburb that has been the centre of the US film industry since 1911. If the script required a cityscape, San Francisco often stepped into the role. In the course of the 20th century it matured into a venerable screen-star, inspiring many famous directors and providing spectacular backdrops for everything from *film noir* thrillers to TV commercials.

One satisfaction of watching old movies starring San Francisco is how instantly recognisable the city is. Cable cars, the skyscrapers of the Financial District, Alcatraz, the Golden Gate and Bay Bridges – all seem as potent in scratchy black and white as they do in living colour. In particular, 1940s crime films such *as The Maltese Falcon* and *Dark Passage*, both starring Humphrey Bogart, and Alfred Hitchcock's 1958 *Vertigo*, have left an ominous mood hanging in its streets.

The notorious prison on Alcatraz has inspired an entire mini-series that includes Burt Lancaster's *Bird Man of Alcatraz* (1962), Clint Eastwood's *Escape from Alcatraz* (1979) and the more recent *The Rock* (1996).

Chinatown became a particularly popular location in the 1980s, appearing in films such as *Hammett*, *Dim Sum* and *The Dead Pool*. Other notable films exploiting areas of the city include *Presidio*, *Pacific Heights* and *Bullitt*, which used its switchback hills to create the ultimate city car chase.

Barely a month goes by without a movie being shot here, a creative centre for the film industry in its own right. The evidence? Crews may have streets blocked off, day or night, and even Victorian buildings are stars – a family home in Pacific Heights featured in *Mrs Doubtfire* (1993). The director and producer Francis Ford Coppola has his Amercian Zoetrupe production and

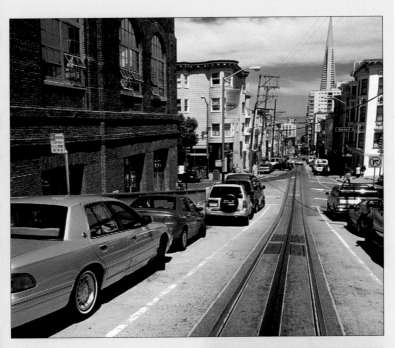

post-production companies in the copper-clad Columbus Tower. North of the city near San Rafael the director George Lucas, creator of *Star Wars* and the Indiana Jones films, has facilities in Lucas Valley and is building a digital arts centre in the Presidio. Clearly, San Francisco is one actor that will never be out of work.

Facing page: The Golden Gate Bridge is a prominent background feature in *Vertigo*
Above: The sloping streets provide great locations for car chases
Right: Coppola's post-production facilities are housed in the copper-clad building on the right

ANNUAL EVENTS
January/February
San Francisco's annual conga of ethnic festivals kicks off with the celebrations for **Chinese New Year** – dates vary according to the lunar calendar. The main events take place in Chinatown, ablaze with firecrackers and Good Luck banners, and include the **Miss Chinatown USA** beauty contest and a **Golden Dragon Parade** down Market Street to Union Square on the final Saturday night.

March
Irish roots are honoured on **St Patrick's Day** with church services, a good drink and a big flag-waving parade along Market Street on 17 March or the nearest Sunday. Though not an official government holiday, Easter is celebrated by many San Franciscans.

April
San Francisco's Japanese community holds its Northern California **Cherry Blossom Festival** in the latter half of the month, with performances by artists from the mother country and a parade staged in Japantown. The **San Francisco International Film Festival**, the oldest in North America, invades the city's cinemas.

May
On 5 May **Cinco de Mayo** remembers the Mexican victory at Puebla in 1862 over the French. Festivities are held on the nearest weekend and culminate with the crowning of a fiesta queen in the Civic Center. At the end of the month the Mission district lets rip with a Rio-style **Carnaval** featuring costumed parades, Latin sounds and crafts and food stalls. The **Bay to Breakers** race sees costumed crowds running between the Bay and Ocean Beach.

June
The last Sunday finds the **Lesbian Gay Bisexual Transgender Pride Celebration Parade** whistling and waving its way down a Market Street lined with rainbow flags. **Gay Pride Week** and the **San Francisco International Lesbian Gay Bisexual Transgender Film Festival** are also held this month. Neighbourhood street fairs take place in Union Street, Haight (Ashbury) Street and North Beach.

July
The **Fourth of July**, Independence Day, is marked with a public holiday and fireworks galore by Crissy Field and on Golden Gate Bridge. **Cable Car Bell-Ringing Contest** is held in Union Square. Local talent is featured in the **North Beach Jazz Festival**.

August/September
August brings on the **Nihonmachi (Japantown) Street Fair**. In September is the free **Comedy Day** in Golden Gate Park and **Folsom Street Fair** in SOMA, which attracts alternative lifestyle communities, especially the leather set. On the last weekend, the **San Francisco Blues Festival** is staged at Fort Mason Great Meadow.

October
12 October is **Columbus Day**, commemorating the Genoan explorer's

discovery of the New World in 1492, celebrated in style by the Italian community in North Beach. Traditional festivities include services in the Church of Saints Peter and Paul in Washington Square and a parade to Fisherman's Wharf for the blessing of the fishing fleet. The **Castro Street Fair** and (US Navy) **Fleet Week** are other events. **Halloween** is a big excuse to party – a large section of the Castro District is blocked off for a street party in cross-gender fantasy costumes, and exhibitionists let it all hang out at the **Exotic Erotic Ball**.

November
On 2 November the Mexican community remembers the **Día de los Muertos** (Day of the Dead), when the spirits of their ancestors return, with a nocturnal procession in the Mission. The **San Francisco Jazz Festival** normally takes place in the first fortnight. On the fourth Thursday of the month, **Thanksgiving** is an official holiday recalling the Pilgrim Fathers' first harvest in Massachusetts in 1621, and an unofficial cue for Christmas shopping to begin.

December
Christmas in San Francisco is celebrated with elaborate displays in department-store windows, carol services, performances of *The Nutcracker* by the San Francisco Ballet and a feast of present-buying and family gatherings. As in all good party towns, **New Year's Eve** is a cause of midnight madness and fireworks followed by a public holiday the next day.

Dates of some events change year to year. Contact the San Francisco Visitor Information Center for exact details.

Dragon and dragon dancers in the annual San Francisco Chinese New Year Parade

Children

With its Big City feel and abundant parks, beaches and amusements, San Francisco is ideal for a family holiday. Along with its well-publicised cable cars, ferries and waterfront attractions, there are stimulating museums and unique historical sights to make this a memorable city for children to visit.

Open-air learning at the Maritime Historic Park

Babysitting
Hotels can usually arrange babysitting services. Check *www.gocitykids.com* for listings of babysitters, day care and other resources.

Beaches
See p129.

Essentials
Parents bringing children or babies to San Francisco have little to worry about. The high standard of living in California means that all necessary supplies and medical services are to hand, including nappies (diapers), baby food and formula milk. If you need to hire a car seat for a child, double check availability when making the booking. Strollers (buggies) can be hired from some bike rental shops.

Hotels
In their competitive search for custom, many hotels have introduced elaborate children's programmes. These can range from welcoming goody bags and enrolment in a Kids' Club to the provision of child-size dressing gowns, free books and games, and – perhaps– the installation of a miniature piano for your budding Mozart. Before making a reservation, always ask how a hotel plans to make your darling(s) feel regal, and enquire about whether kids stay or eat free or whether there are any discount programmes.

Museums
Those of particular appeal to the young are the California Academy of Sciences, the Exploratorium, a hands-on science lab with the Tactile Dome (*see pp36–7 & p52*), and the Randall Museum (*199 Museum Way. Tel: (415) 554 9600; www.randall/museum.org. Open: Tue–Sat 10am–5pm. Free admission*), with ceramic workshops and animal feedings on Saturday. Age limits vary between museums for free or discounted admission for children.

Bay Area Discovery Museum
Adventure museum with arts, performance and science activities, including a San Francisco Bay hall where children can man a fishing boat and crawl through an undersea tunnel. There is a café, picnic area and fine views of the Golden Gate Bridge – allow half a day. *On the north side of Golden Gate Bridge, take the Alexander Ave exit. 557*

McReynolds Rd, East Fort Baker.
Tel: (415) 339 3900;
www.baykidsmuseum.org. Open: Tue–Fri
9am–4pm, Sat–Sun 10am–5pm.
Admission charge (free second Sat of
every month).

Playgrounds

Opened in 1888, the Children's
Playground in Golden Gate Park is the
oldest in America in a public park.
There are others in Washington Square
(North Beach), Portsmouth Square and
Yerba Buena Gardens (*see individual*
entries).

Zeum

Entertainment centre atop Moscone
Convention Center with a vintage
carousel, bowling complex, skating rink,
theatre and interactive museum
designed for children.
4th St and Howard St. Tel: (415) 820
3320; www.zeum.org
Open Tue–Sun 11am–5pm, summer,
Wed in school term.
Admission charge.

What Now?
San Francisco
Alcatraz *See pp31–3.*
Boat trips *See p130.*
Cable Car Barn *See p36.*
Golden Gate Park *See p62.*
Hyde Street Pier (historic ships) *See p70.*
Pier 39 (Fisherman's Wharf) *See p83.*
San Francisco Zoo *See pp90–91.*

Around the Bay
Coyote Point Museum for Environmental
Education (San Mateo) *See p121.*
Six Flags Marine World *See p115.*
Paramount's Great America *See p119.*
Winchester Mystery House *See pp120–21.*

Restaurants

Fast-food outlets mean that hunger
pangs are easily satiated, and there are
many family-orientated restaurants with
highchairs, child portions and even
tabletop amusements.

Transport

On MUNI and BART under-fives travel
free. Discount fares apply for ages 5–12
(BART) and under 17s (MUNI).

There are all sorts of fun activities at Fisherman's
Wharf

Sport and leisure

Whether you like to play it, watch it or just keep healthy, sport is a great way to observe and enjoy the American way of life.

Take me out to the ball game

American football

The San Francisco 49ers are the only team to have won the Super Bowl five times – the most recent was in 1994. Home games are played on Sunday afternoons between September and December at Monster Park. Their popularity means that getting tickets for big games can be difficult.
13km (8 miles) south on Highway 101 at Candlestick Point. www.49ers.com. Ticket information: Tel: (415) 656 4900. Games normally start at 1.15pm. A special MUNI bus service operates on game days. www.sfmuni.com/football

Baseball

The San Francisco Giants are in the National League and play home games between April and October at AT & T Park.
24 Willie Mays Plaza. Tel: (415) 972 2000; www.sfgiants.com. MUNI: N-Line. Bus: 10, 15, 30, 45, 47. Additional bus and streetcar service before and after games; www.sfmuni.com/baseball. Ferry service: Golden Gate Ferry.

The Oakland Athletics (the A's) are one of America's most successful baseball teams and are in the American League. Home games are played at the McAfee Coliseum.
66th Ave & Hegenberger Rd (off Interstate 880). Tel: (510) 638 4900;
http://.oakland.athletics.mlb.com BART: Coliseum.

Basketball

The NBA Golden State Warriors play at The (Oakland Coliseum) Arena October through April.
66th Ave & Hegenberger Rd (off Interstate 880). Tel: (510) 986 2200; www.nba.com/warriors BART: Coliseum.

Cycling

See p128.

Sea fishing

Take a wander around the sports fishing boats moored in Jefferson Lagoon, Fisherman's Wharf, to find out what trips are on offer according to the season. Expeditions leave very early in the morning and take the best part of the day, with add-on prices for rod rental, day licence and equipment. Salmon, bass and halibut are the most likely catch. Ten sport fishing boats depart daily.

Fitness centres

Major business-orientated hotels often have their own gym and fitness facilities, or an arrangement enabling guests to use those of a nearby club. They will also have suggested jogging routes in the immediate area.

Club One
Fitness facilities and classes.
Multiple locations.
www.clubone.com
YMCA of San Francisco
With 11 San Francisco locations,
it's easy to stay fit.
Tel: (415) 777 9622;
www.ymcasf.org

Golf
In addition to five public San Francisco
golf courses there are many private ones
in the Bay Area.
Gleneagles Golf Club
9 holes.
2100 Sunnydale Ave
Tel: (415) 587 2425.
Golden Gate Park
9 holes.
47th Ave & Fulton St.
Tel: (415) 751 8987.
Harding Park
Fleming and Harding courses,
27 holes each.
Harding Rd near Skyline Blvd.
Tel: (415) 664 4690.
Lincoln Park
18 holes.
34th Ave & Clement St.
Tel: (415) 221 9911.

Horse racing
Bay Meadows Race Track
Thoroughbred race meetings are held
between August and June at this San
Mateo course, with daily races from
Wednesday to Sunday.
2600 South Delaware St, San Mateo
(20 miles south off US 101 at Highway 92).
Tel: (650) 574 7223;
www.baymeadows.com

Golden Gate Fields
Opened in 1941, Golden Gate Fields
is east across San Francisco Bay.
Thoroughbred race meetings are held
August through May, with daily races
Wednesday to Sunday.
1100 Eastshore Highway (Off US 80),
Albany. Tel: (510) 559 7300;
www.goldengatefields.com

Horse riding
Golden Gate Park Stables
These historic stables in Golden Gate
Park are being rebuilt and are
temporarily closed. Riding trails remain
open for those with their own mounts.
John F Kennedy Drive & 36th Ave.
Miwok Stables
Enjoy the Marin Headlands on
horseback.
Tennessee Valley, Marin Headlands.
Tel: (415) 383 8048;
www.miwokstables.com
Sea Horse Ranch
Ride the beaches of Half Moon Bay.
1828 Cabrillo Highway.
Tel: (650) 726 2362, (650) 726 9903;
www.horserentals.com

Monster Park
Built in 1960, this sporting venue can hold
60,000 spectators and is notoriously chilly,
windy and often foggy. Until Pacific Bell Park
was built in 2000 for baseball, Candlestick
Park (now AT & T Park), as Monster Park was
then, was shared by the San Francisco's
49ers football team and the Giants baseball
team. A baseball game was in progress
between the Giants and the Oakland A's
when the Loma Prieta earthquake struck on
17 October 1989 – one reason why there
were relatively few casualties. As one
reporter quipped, 'this was the first time a
stadium, not the fans, did The Wave.'

Kayaking

Sea Trek Ocean Kayaking Center

Escorted half- and full-day trips along
San Francisco and Sausalito waterfronts
in single or double kayaks. Departures
from Schoonmaker Point Marina,
Sausalito.
PO Box 1987, Sausalito.
Tel: (415) 488 1000;
www.seatrekkayak.com

Motor sports

Infineon Raceway is the nearest
racetrack at the southern end of the
Sonoma Valley. Motor sports events take
place 340 days each year and every
weekend.
At the junction of Highways 37 and 121.
Tel: (800) 870 8223;
www.infineonraceway.com

Roller-skating

Roller-skaters and roller-bladers are
dynamic features of San Francisco's
streets and parks. If you want to join
this urban disco, boots and protective
gear can be rented from vans beside
Ocean Beach and specialist shops.
Golden Gate Park Skate & Bike
3038 Fulton St. Tel: (415) 668 1117.

Running

San Francisco hosts many events
intended to make running seem like
communal fun rather than a self-
punishing chore. The Bay to Breakers
Foot Race, held in late May, is a
costumed fun run from The
Embarcadero to Ocean Beach via Golden
Gate Park that attracts thousands of
entrants. The more serious San Francisco
Marathon takes place in late July and
starts on the Golden Gate Bridge. Other
runs include Run to the Far Side in
Golden Gate Park in November.

If you like to go jogging, the Golden
Gate Promenade is a scenic shoreline
route, and Golden Gate Park is another
popular venue.

Sailing

The yachting season traditionally starts
with a splendid taking to the waters at
the end of April. The best way to
investigate boat hire or joining a sailing
trip is to visit the marinas at South
Beach Harbor and across in Sausalito.

Adventure Cat Sailing Charters

Career around Alcatraz, Angel Island
and Sausalito on a sailing catamaran
from March–November.
Pier 39, J dock.
Tel: (415) 777 1630, (800) 498 4228;
www.adventurecat.com

Cass' Marina

Sailing tuition and rental.
*1702 Bridgeway, Sausalito. Tel: (415) 332
6789, (800) 472 4595;*
www.cassmarina.com

Rendezvous Charters/Spinnaker Sailing

Sailing boats of all sizes with or without
skipper.
Pier 40, South Beach Marina.
Tel: (415) 543 7333;
www.rendezvouscharters.com

Spas

Sunset Sauna and Massage

Individual or group sauna or massage
near Golden Gate Park.
1214 20th Ave (at Lincoln Way).
Tel: (415) 753 2559, (800) 200 2559;
www.sunsetsauna.com

Kabuki Springs & Spa
Japanese spa with *shiatsu* and Swedish
massage and communal baths.
1750 Geary Blvd, Japantown. Tel: (415)
922 6000; www.kabukisprings.com

Swimming
Beware! The waters around San
Francisco are often cold, with strong
currents making swimming unsafe. If
you want a dip, the best place in the city
is China Beach (*see p129*), or drive north
to Stinson Beach. Aquatic Park is
another popular bathing spot. Public
swimming pools are administered by the
San Francisco Recreation and Parks
Department. For more information:
http://216.103.100.45/ParRecFacilities.

Tennis
The San Francisco Recreation and Parks
Department provides over 100 tennis

courts around the city for free use.
Ask at your hotel for the nearest courts.
For more information:
http://216.103.100.45/ParRecFacilities.

Golden Gate Park
Twenty-one tennis courts are available
in Golden Gate Park for a small fee.
These can be reserved at weekends.
Tel: (415) 831 6301.
San Francisco Tennis Club
Private tennis facilities in the SOMA
district.
645 5th St. Tel: (415) 777 9000;
www.sftennis.com

Windsurfing
Cityfront Boardsports
Lessons and equipment rental on offer.
Closed in winter.
2936 Lyon St. Tel: (415) 929 7873;
www.boardsports.com

Sailing round the Bay; an enjoyable pastime

Food and drink

Ditch the diet. Load the wallet. Summon the taste buds. You're in San Francisco, the ambassador of Californian and diverse ethnic cuisines, where eating out is a passion and restaurants attract a level of impetuous talent and client fanaticism normally reserved for the world of high fashion.

Sourdough bread is a San Francisco speciality

Californian cuisine

The word most food critics reach for when asked to describe California's cuisine is 'eclectic'. Like the region itself, culinary enterprise here is a wilfully progressive fusion of past, present and foreign styles. Classic French, new Asian, modern British, Mom's apple pie – if it tastes thrilling, who cares about titles?

Dine your way around the world; Mexican taqueria in the Haight

The Bay Area's gastronomic reputation dates from the late 1970s, when chefs fell into step with a growing desire for healthy yet sensation-rich living. Inspired by foreign travel and the state's diverse and abundant produce, they took to using ultra-fresh ingredients to create dishes that would startle the palate, delight the eye – and please the nutritionist.

The result is a foodie heaven, featuring iconoclastic celebrity chefs, see-it-all restaurants, *nouvelle cuisine* portions on art school crockery, waiters as mellifluous as sycophantic courtiers, menus that read like multilingual crossword clues – and damn good food in a fun world. San Francisco loves all this – if you want to know a good place to eat, just find half an hour, a comfortable seat, and a San Franciscan.

Dining ethnic

San Francisco really does offer the world on a plate. Few tourists leave without a meal in its two busiest dining venues, Chinatown and oh-so-Italian North Beach, but the possibilities seem limited only by one's capacity for research. Russian, Japanese, Cambodian, Korean, Mesopotamian, Moroccan, Ethiopian,

Indian, Mexican, Greek and Swedish are some of the tastes that await the global gourmet. There are vegetarian eateries, and most restaurant menus include nourishing vegetarian – and sometimes vegan – dishes.

What to eat and when

The possibilities are dazzling – in San Francisco even the theoretically simple task of ordering a sandwich turns into a brain-damaging multiple-choice interrogation.

To do things properly, breakfast should either be taken in a diner with an all-American fry-up of eggs, bacon, hash browns and bits of fruit, or in a café with a coffee and croissants. Sunday means the mighty *San Francisco Chronicle* double-size issue and brunch (where breakfast blends with lunch), to include a Bloody Mary or a sparkling wine-orange juice mimosa.

Lunch menus are lighter and cheaper than those for dinner, and there is a relentless supply of takeaways, fast food and 24-hour delis to fill in the gaps. San Francisco's grander hotels have afternoon tea, served *à l'anglais* with Earl Grey, scones and bone china.

San Franciscan specialities

All visitors racing over the Golden Gate Bridge are assumed to be panting to try Dungeness crab and sourdough bread. The crabs are harvested in the Bay between mid-November and June and sold in stalls and restaurants on Fisherman's Wharf, along with a treasury of

seafood including lobster, prawns, shrimps, clams and abalone.

Sourdough bread is a white, crusty loaf with a tangy flavour that was a staple food in the gold rush days. Unlike the yeast-based baking of today, it uses a starter culture that the miners would take with them on their travels – the term 'sourdough' was once used to describe anyone who had spent a winter in Alaska, a legacy of the 1890s Klondike Gold Rush.

Hungry? Fisherman's Wharf is the place to go for seafood

Drinks

Alcoholic drinks can only be bought and consumed by people over 21 years old. If you look young, you may be asked to prove your age by showing some form of photo ID.

Beer

The locally made brew is Anchor Steam Beer (book the free tour in advance, *tel: (415) 863 8350; www.anchorbrewing. com*). Specialist bars and restaurants also sell beer made by microbreweries like Gordon Biersch and the San Francisco Brewing Company. Other Californian beers of distinction are Sierra Nevada Ale and Red Tail Ale.

Wine

When in California, drink Californian wine (*see p166–7*). The mark-up on bottles served in restaurants is high, so imbibing is best seen as a delicious and necessary learning curve.

Waiters are expected to be knowledgeable about the wines they serve, so quiz them relentlessly. Wines are usually listed by grape variety rather than region – those from the Hess, Landmark and Stag's Leap wineries are a good starting point.

Non-alcoholic drinks

Prepare for a complex choice of fruit juices and smoothies, fizzy drinks, milk in varying shades of fatlessness, herbal and fruit teas and a splendidly epicurean coffee scene.

Water

Tap water is safe to drink, but many health-conscious San Franciscans prefer bottled mineral water. Calistoga, from the Napa Valley, is a popular local brand.

Bars

Bars are open at various times between early morning and 2am depending on their location and clientele. The choice runs from sports-mad bars and serious drinkers' dives to yuppie wine bars and rooftop nightclubs. A cocktail on the top floor of a swish hotel, with the lights of the city and Bay spread below like a blanket of jewels, is a very San Franciscan pleasure. Many bars have a Happy Hour, usually 5–7pm.

Carnelian Room

On the 52nd floor with a 40,000-bottle wine cellar.
555 California St. Tel: (415) 433 7500.

Bottle and glass of Anchor Steam Beer from San Francisco's oldest brewery

Poetry readings are essential to café culture

Gordon Biersch
Trendy microbrewery serving German-style beers made on the premises.
2 Harrison St. at the Embarcadero.
Tel: (415) 243 8246.

Hurricane Bar
Grass-roofed huts, mock thunderstorms and live music in the Tonga Room of the Fairmont Hotel.
950 Mason St. Tel: (415) 772 5278.

Pied Piper Bar
Maxfield Parrish's 1909 painting of *The Pied Piper* ignites this clubby bar at The Palace Hotel.
2 New Montgomery St.
Tel: (415) 512 1111.

Redwood Room
Art Deco redwood panelling, Klimt prints and piano music at the Clift Hotel.
495 Geary St. Tel: (415) 775 4700.

San Francisco Brewing Company
Wood floors, real ale and pub atmosphere.
155 Columbus Ave. Tel: (415) 434 3344.

Top of the Mark
Legendary 19th-floor cocktail bar atop the Inter-Continental Mark Hopkins Hotel on Nob Hill.
California and Mason sts.
Tel: (415) 392 3434.

Vesuvio
An original Beat Generation boozer.
255 Columbus Ave. Tel: (415) 362 3370.

Cafés
Atlas Café
A blue-collar and counter-culture clientele, evening entertainment and vegan and non-vegan menus.
3049 20th St at Alabama St (Mission District). Tel: (415) 648 1047.

Brain Wash
Combined launderette, café, and live music nightly except Thur, in SOMA.
1122 Folsom St.
Tel: (415) 861 3663.

Café de la Presse
Lively café/restaurant selling foreign newspapers and magazines.
469 Bush St at Grant Ave.
Tel: (415) 398 2680.

Caffè Trieste
Traditional North Beach haunt for literary bohemians, with occasional Saturday opera.
601 Vallejo St. Tel: (415) 392 6739.

Caffè Trinity
Coffee and complex Italian sandwiches near the Civic Center.
1 Trinity Center, 1145 Market St.
Tel: (415) 864 3333.

Canvas Café and Gallery
Local visual artists' work hangs on the walls, and laptop-toters hang out for hours. Nightly entertainment, across from Golden Gate Park.
1200 9th Ave at Lincoln Way.
Tel: (415) 504 0060.

Cole Valley Café
Laid-back coffeehouse in the Haight.
701 Cole St at Waller St.
Tel: (415) 668 5282.

Mario's Bohemian Cigar Store Café
Watch Washington Square go by.
566 Columbus Ave.
Tel: (415) 362 0536.

San Francisco has some of the most densely populated neighbourhoods in the US and some of the easiest escapes from the urban crush. A local favourite is Marin County, just north across the Golden Gate Bridge. By ferry to Sausalito or Tiburon, by bicycle across the bridge, by car to the wilds of Point Reyes, Marin offers long beaches (and frigid waters), elegant meals overlooking the bay, sweaty slogs up mountain slopes and shady redwood groves.

Sausalito began as a 19th-century summer resort for San Francisco that became a 1950s haven for artists, Beats, and poets who tired of big-city life. Much of the town centre is a National Historic Landmark District focused on the Spanish-style Plaza de Viña del Mar and sculptured elephants rescued from the 1915 Panama-Pacific International Exposition. The best bay views and view restaurants are along Bridgeway, walking south from the ferry landing.

Tiburon was once the terminus for a railway ferry to San Francisco. Today, it is famed for sweeping bay views and an almost-always sunny waterfront. Restaurants and outdoor decks surrounding the ferry landing are popular mealtime excursions from the city.

West Marin is more rural. The Golden Gate Bridge leads straight to the Marin Headlands, a former military reservation that is now part of the Golden Gate National Recreation Area. Just north of GGNRA is Muir Woods National Monument,

a tiny remnant of the vast redwood forests that once covered most of coastal Northern California. The 224-hectare (554-acre) grove is nestled beneath Mount Tamalpais, the highest point in Marin County at 784m (2,571 ft). Farther north lie the curving beaches and inland valleys of Point Reyes National Seashore that are popular with hikers, mountain bikers and horse riders.

Facing page: elephant statue lamp in town square, Sausalito, originally created for the 1915 Panama-Pacific International Exposition Above: headlands and beach at Point Reyes National Seashore; right: Redwood trees at Muir Woods National Monument

Where to eat

The San Francisco restaurant scene is a success-hungry world of trailblazing chefs, cutting-edge designers and venues that rise and fall like hit records. Dining at the latest hot spot in the midst of a buzzing in-crowd is a very San Franciscan excitement, but don't be dismayed to find it's booked solid for months. There are an estimated 2,499 other restaurants in the city and many of them are worth your money.

Chinatown and North Beach are rewarding areas to explore if you like a menu-browsing wander. It is a good idea to make a note of restaurants you meet on your travels – many produce photocopied menus you can take away for perusal. Don't be put off by the idea of dining in the better hotels. Many employ name chefs who have worked their way through a fiercely competitive world, and the service is usually faultless.

Vegetarian and vegan menu items are not uncommon – be sure to enquire when booking, and quiz servers about ingredients before ordering.

The listing below suggests something of the variety available. Local papers and their online sites have restaurant reviews. Word-of-mouth is especially relevant in a city where many people eat out several times a week, and its compact nature makes it worth travelling a little to get the best. Isolate your target and make a reservation. Many restaurants can be booked online at *www.opentable.com*

The symbols below are an indication of restaurant prices. The ★ sign represents the approximate cost of a three-course dinner per person with tax but not alcohol or tip. Lunchtime prices are often less.

★	under $20
★★	under $30
★★★	over $30

Tax of 8.5 per cent is added to bills in San Francisco. Tips are not usually included and should be 15–20 per cent.

It is always safer to take a taxi home at night.

Afternoon sidewalk traffic at Calzone's Restaurant, North Beach, San Francisco

Annabelle's Bar and Bistro ★★★
This classic San Francisco restaurant is convenient to Yerba Buena Gardens, with an oyster bar, pizzas, meat and fish entrées and great service.
68 4th St. SOMA.
Tel: (415) 777 1200.
www.annabelles.net

Ana Mandara ★★★
Traditional Vietnamese recipes and classic French preparation create an exquisite Vietnamese restaurant in San Francisco despite its touristy location in Ghirardelli Square.
891 Beach St at Polk St.
Tel: (415) 771 6800.
www.anamandara.com

Anzu ★★★
This Nikko Hotel restaurant offers the city's best combination of *sushi* and grilled beef, preferably washed down by *sake* martinis.
222 Mason St.
Tel: (415) 394 1100.
www.restaurantanzu.com

Bacar Restaurant and Wine Salon ★★★
Succulent Mediterranean flavours weave through Californian, French and Italian menu items, backed by a multistorey-wall wine cellar.
448 Brannan St. SOMA
Tel: (415) 904 4100.
www.bacarsf.com

Bix ★★★
Art Deco interior, live piano or jazz and traditional American fare make a winning recipe.
56 Gold St. Jackson Square.
Tel: (415) 433 6300.
www.bixrestaurant.com

Boulevard ★★★
A far-ranging menu and a wilfully Continental *belle époque* decor create Paris by the Bay.
Embarcadero. 1 Mission St at Steuart St. Tel: (415) 543 6084. www. boulevardrestaurant.com

Brandy Ho's Hunan Food★
Spicy Chinese cooking from Hunan province.
North Beach.
217 Columbus Ave.
Tel: (415) 788 7527.

Calzone's ★★
Pizzas, classic Italian dishes and picture-window views of Columbus Avenue.
North Beach.
430 Columbus Ave.
Tel: (415) 397 3600.
www.calzonesf.com

Cha Cha Cha ★★
Cooking with a Caribbean-Cajun twist and exotic shrines on the walls.
Haight-Ashbury.
1801 Haight St. at Shrader St. Tel: (415) 386 7670.

Citizen Thai and the Monkey★★
The 'Citizen' side has a nuanced menu in the midst of Buddhas; the 'Monkey' section has Thai street food to go, atop noodles or rice.
1268 Grant Ave at Vallejo Street
Tel: (415) 364 0007
www.citizenthai.com

City View ★
Chinese *dim-sum* in a spacious, spotless world.
Chinatown.
662 Commercial St.
Tel: (415) 398 2838.

Equinox ★★
Revolving restaurant on the roof of the Hyatt Regency Hotel, serving dinner Wednesday to Sunday.
5 Embarcadero Center.
Tel: (415) 788 1234.

Farallon ★★★
One of the city's hottest seafood restaurants with jellyfish chandeliers!
450 Post St.
Tel: (415) 956 6969. www. farallonrestaurant.com

Fly Trap ★★
Bentwood chairs, white tablecloths, traditional San Franciscan dishes, satisfied grins, and a century of history.
SOMA.
606 Folsom St off 2nd St.
Tel: (415) 243 0580.

http://flytraprestaurant.com
Closed: Sat lunchtime
& Sun.

Fog City Diner ★★
Californian cuisine in a
restaurant resembling a
chrome-faced railroad
dining car.
Embarcadero.
1300 Battery St.
Tel: (415) 982 2000.
www.fogcitydiner.com

Fournou's Ovens ★★★
Gourmet American

cuisine in the snug
comforts of the
Renaissance Stanford
Court Hotel.
Nob Hill.
905 California St.
Tel: (415) 989 1910.

Gordon Biersch ★★
Tasty California dining in
a warehouse turned
microbrewery.
Embarcadero.
2 Harrison St.
Tel: (415) 243 8246.

*www.gordonbiersch.
com/restaurants*

Greens ★★
Top-class vegetarian
cuisine combined with
stunning Bay views.
Fort Mason Center.
*Building A. Marina Blvd
at Buchanan St.*
Tel: (415) 771 6222.
www.greensrestaurant.com

Il Fornaio ★★
Constantly popular
restaurant and speciality
bread shop offering
definitive Italian fare.
North Embarcadero.
1265 Battery St.
Tel: (415) 986 0100.
www.ilfornaio.com

**India Garden
Restaurant** ★
Delicious Indian home
cooking in an easy-going
atmosphere. SOMA.
1261 Folsom St at 8th St.
Tel: (415) 626 2798.

John's Grill ★★★
Cosy, photo-lined
chophouse, mentioned
in Dashiell Hammett's
The Maltese Falcon.
Downtown.
63 Ellis St.
Tel: (415) 986 3274.
Closed: Sun lunchtime.
http://johnsgrill.com

LuLu ★★★
Thought-about
Californian cuisine in a
buzzing, in-crowd
atmosphere.

Tadich Grill, founded in 1849, is located on California Street and is
the oldest restaurant in San Francisco

SOMA.
816 Folsom St.
Tel: (415) 495 5775.
www.restaurantlulu.com
**McCormick and
Kuleto's ★★**
Superlative choice of
seafood complemented by
splendid views of the Bay.
Ghirardelli Square.
900 North Point St.
Tel: (888) 344 6861, (415)
929 1730. www.mccormick
andschmicks.com
Millennium*
Vegetarian cuisine in the
heart of the Union Square
theatre district lures
carnivores, too.
580 Geary St.
Tel: (415) 345 3900. www.
millenniumrestaurant.com
MoMo's ★
Traditional American fare
with a Californian twist,
a favourite with local
politicos.
760 Second St. SOMA.
Tel: (415) 227 8660.
www.sfmomos.com
Mooses ★★★
Contemporary Italian
cuisine and a big, happy
atmosphere.
Washington Square.
1652 Stockton St.
Tel: (800) 286 6673, (415)
989 7800.
www.mooses.com
Pane e Vino ★★
Stylish Italian trattoria,
good for pasta or fish.

715 Union St.
Tel: (415) 346 2111.
www.panevinofrasoria.com
**Park Chalet Garden
Restaurant ★**
Sandwiches, salads and
entrées, beneath a glass
roof at the western end of
Golden Gate Park.
1000 Great Highway at
Ocean Beach. Sunset
District.
Tel: (415) 386 8439.
www.beachchalet.com
Silks ★★★
Heavenly Californian-
Asian cuisine at the
Mandarin Oriental Hotel
– among the best
gourmet dining in town.
Financial District.
222 Sansome St.
Tel: (415) 986 2020.
www.mandarinoriental.com
Slanted Door ★★★
Superb Vietnamese
cuisine with fresh local
ingredients, served in a
bright, noisy atmosphere.
1 Ferry Building, No. 3.
Tel: (415) 861 8032.
www.slanteddoor.com
Stinking Rose ★★
Paradise for garlic-lovers,
where 'it's chic to reek'.
North Beach.
325 Columbus Ave.
Tel: (415) 781 7673.
www.thestinkingrose.com
Suppenkuche ★★
Home-style German
food near City Hall.

525 Laguna St at
Hayes St.
Tel: (415) 252 9289.
www.suppenkuche.com
Tadich Grill ★★
San Franciscan no-
reservations institution
serving dependable fish
and seafood in a world of
shiny wood and white
linen.
240 California St.
Tel: (415) 391 1849.
The Terrace ★★★
The Ritz-Carlton Hotel's
informal restaurant
has the best and most
sheltered outdoor dining
in San Francisco. Don't
miss the Sunday Jazz
Brunch.
600 Stockton St at
California St.
Tel: (415) 773 6198.
www.ritzcarlton.com
Yank Sing ★
Perfect for *dim sum* lunch
adventures – reservations
essential.
One Rincon Center.
101 Spear St at
Mission St.
Tel: (415) 957 9300.
www.yanksing.com
Zuni Café ★★★
A French and Italian
institution, ideal
for hunger pangs if
visiting the Hayes
Valley.
1658 Market St.
Tel: (415) 552 2522.

Californian wine

The Spanish missionaries introduced grapevines to California, but winemaking only became a major enterprise after the gold rush. The Buena Vista winery in Sonoma, founded in 1857 by a Hungarian count, claims to be the oldest commercial vineyard in the region. Today more than 90 per cent of American wine comes from California, with the best produced in more than 400 flagship wineries lining the Napa and Sonoma valleys.

California viticulture is a tale of European arts tuned to a New World. Settlers from France, Italy, Germany and Eastern Europe imported vine stocks and expertise from their native lands, adapting varieties to suit local soils and fog-bound microclimates.

The greatest part of the Napa and Sonoma vineyards is today given over to producing white Chardonnays and red Cabernet Sauvignons. Zinfandel,

a red grape unique to California, is grown extensively in Sonoma.

As winemakers seek new challenges, there is increased diversity – white wines like Chenin Blanc, Sauvignon Blanc and Riesling, and reds such as Merlot and Pinot Noir, are now common varieties. Sparkling wine producers such as Mumm, Taitlinger, Roederer, and Moët & Chandon have also started successful ventures here.

The international success of Californian wine dates from the 1970s, but despite a phenomenal demand from European markets, Californians still have to work hard to educate their compatriots in the pleasures of imbibing. Wines have been promoted by grape type rather than place of origin but that is changing: California has 93 of 165 American Viticultural Areas. There is a healthy rivalry between dynastic wine families and new 'wine brats'. While the former are keen to preserve the measured and conservative disciplines of the old school, the latter go in for funky labels, pop-industry-style publicity and crusades against wine snobbery. 'We make wines that WE like to drink' raps one iconoclastic winery. 'Then we set out to find people who like what we like.'

Facing page: Californian white wines
Right: bottle of Kenwood Cabernet Sauvignon from grapes grown in the Jack London vineyard, once owned and worked by writer Jack London
Below: The sign says it all

Hotels and accommodation

San Francisco has been putting visitors up for the night since the gold rush, and has a spectacular choice of hotels and other accommodation to please all tastes and budgets.

Most hotels in San Francisco are Downtown

Where to stay

San Francisco is a city of hills, vistas and large, skyscraping hotels. If you don't mind heights and high-speed lifts that transplant your stomach to your mouth, there is no better place to stay than on the zillionth floor of a historic hotel with picture-window views out to the Bay and its famous bridges.

Most visitors stay in Downtown, on Nob Hill and at Fisherman's Wharf, which are all close to the main sights. Anywhere else will be more relaxed, but may require some travelling in order to reach points of interest. The San Francisco Convention and Visitors Bureau produces a *Visitor Planning Guide* that includes comprehensive details about all types of accommodation available in the city and Bay Area, answers queries at *(888) 782 9673*, and provides an online booking service for some accommodation at its website, *www.sfvisitor.org http://onlysf.sfvisitor.org/where-to-stay*

Prices

All prices for lodgings in San Francisco are subject to a 'transient occupancy' tax of 14 per cent. Hotel prices are per room at a single or double rate. Always ask about discount rates in large chain hotels, as they never stop having special offers and tariff fluctuations. Booking online may offer a discount. Expect to pay around $125 or more for a good-size, quality room. There is no grading system of hotels by stars as in Europe.

Bills are normally settled by credit card – an imprint will be taken on check-in. Many hotels now have complete 'No Smoking' floors. Breakfast is rarely included in the price of a room. Telephone and parking charges vary considerably from hotel to hotel.

Children

In many cases children sharing with their parents or caregivers are included

The high life

Riding the lifts (elevators) in San Francisco's skyscraping grand hotels can be as thrilling as a funfair ride. Some slide up and down the outside of the building, with glass windows providing sudden and sensational views. The five that rocket up to the 32nd floor of the Tower Building at the Westin St Francis Hotel in Union Square travel at 305m (1,000ft) a minute, and there is similar free fun at The Fairmont Hotel on Nob Hill, where the glass elevator at its east end shoots up 24 storeys. Interior lifts can also be exciting, notably those within the staggering atrium of the Hyatt Regency San Francisco in the Embarcadero Center.

in the room price, but age limits vary from hotel to hotel. Rooms and beds are large compared to those in Europe, with private bathrooms a standard feature.

Reservations

San Francisco is a busy city, so don't be surprised if your favourite hotel is completely filled by bigwigs or members of a pneumatic drill manufacturers' conference. Reservations are normally made by telephoning direct, telephoning a toll-free reservation centre, or booking online. Hotels will usually hold a room reservation until 6pm. You may be charged even if you never occupy a room – if you plan to arrive later, let the hotel or motel know. Chain hotels and discount agencies have their own central reservations numbers. Numbers prefixed *1-800, 888, 877, or 866 are toll-free.*

Best Western
Tel: 800 780 7234; www.bestwestern.com
Central Reservation Service
Tel: 800 555 7555, (407) 740 6442; www.crshotels.com
Holiday Inn
Tel: 800 465 4329; www.ichotelsgroup.com
Hotels.com
Tel: 800 219 4606; www.hotels.com
Hyatt Hotels
Tel: 888 591 1234; www.hyatt.com
Ramada Hotels
Tel: 800 272 6232; www.ramada.com
Starwood Hotels
Tel: 800 598 1753; www.starwoodhotels.com
Travelodge
Tel: 800 578 7878; www.travelodge.com

The San Remo Hotel in North Beach is a restored 1906 Victorian building furnished with antiques

Grand hotels

Many of San Francisco's best-known landmarks are grand hotels, worth visiting for a whiff of history, luxury and ongoing success. You don't need to be a guest to enter – they all have quality restaurants, or just drop by for afternoon tea, a cocktail in the bar or Sunday brunch.

The city's grandest hotel no longer exists. The legendary 800-room, seven-storey Palace Hotel opened in Market Street in 1875, but burned down in the aftermath of the 1906 earthquake. It was imperiously rebuilt on the same site in 1909. Its stained-glass-covered Garden Court restaurant recalls its dignified predecessor.

The **Westin St Francis** in Union Square is an equally venerable hotel, founded in 1904 by the millionaire Crocker family. The ancient Austrian clock in its Powell Street lobby and now in the Tower Lobby was a well-known San Franciscan point of rendezvous. Close by in Geary Street, the **Clift** is

another historic luxury hotel; opened in 1915, its 1934 wood-panelled Redwood Room is an Art Deco masterpiece.

Many more grand hotels gather around Nob Hill. The **Fairmont** in Mason Street opened in 1907, and in nearby Stockton Street the **Ritz-Carlton** boasts the majestic neoclassical 1909 façade of the former Metropolitan Life Insurance building. The **Renaissance Stanford Court Hotel** in California Street occupies a 1912 apartment building, while the purpose-built **Inter-Continental Mark Hopkins**, alias 'The Mark', dates from 1926 and occupies a corner of Nob Hill. Its rooftop cocktail bar, designed by Timothy Pfleuger 13 years later, is a legendary venue for skyscraper partying.

More recent additions to this illustrious lineage include John Portman's innovative 1973 **Hyatt Regency San Francisco** in the Embarcadero Center. He also designed the 21-storey **JW Marriott** (formerly the Pan-Pacific,

1987) in Post Street. **The San Francisco Marriott** in Market Street opened in 1989 and was swiftly christened 'The Jukebox' and 'The Wurlitzer' by locals. The Yerba Buena Gardens arts district added the Four Seasons San Francisco in 2001, and, next to SFMOMA, the St. Regis Hotel San Francisco in 2005. In the Financial District, the **Mandarin Oriental**'s rooms fill the top 11 floors of the fog-piercing 48-storey First Interstate Center, and are as near to heaven as it's safe to go.

Facing page: Lobby of the JW Marriott
Above: The Inter-Continental Mark Hopkins Hotel; right: Hyatt Regency San Francisco Hotel located in Embarcadero Center

Hotels

Art hotels

Small, speciality hotels appealing to an arts, music and media-conscious clientele are a growing feature of the San Francisco hotel scene. Downtown examples include the Hotel Triton, kitted out with zany furniture and contemporary art, the Diva, catering for film crews with sexy décor, and the slickly Italian Hotel Milano in SOMA. The Phoenix Hotel in the Tenderloin is a converted no-tell motel favoured by top rock stars.

Boutique hotels

Distancing themselves from the monster chain hotels catering to business customers and tour groups, boutique hotels are small, individual affairs that usually occupy an historic building and often come kitted out with English country-house comforts. Some like to call themselves 'Inns' to emphasise their logs-on-the-fire individuality. Examples are the waterfront Harbor Court Hotel, Nob Hill Lambourne, and the Kensington Park Hotel near Union Square.

Business hotels

See p175.

Grand hotels

See p170–71.

Motels

Designed as economical pit stops where the passing motorist can get some shut-eye, motels are now being rediscovered as inoffensive bases for a budget holiday. Many of them are lined up along

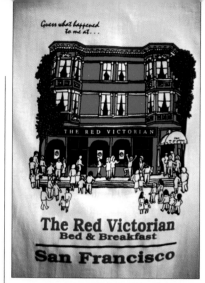

Rooms at the Red Victorian Bed, Breakfast & Art in the Haight are decorated in Sixties style

Lombard Street and include free parking in their rates.

Neighbourhood hotels

You don't have to stay in the whirlpool of the city centre. Every San Francisco neighbourhood has its small local hotels where things are more relaxed and you can get a feel of the community. Examples include the hippy chic Red Victorian Bed, Breakfast & Art in the Haight-Ashbury, the Beat Generation Hotel Bohème in North Beach, the Radisson Miyako in Japantown and the English-flavour Edward II Inn & Suites at the edge of the Marina District.

Bed and breakfast

In America the term 'B&B' does not necessarily signal an inexpensive room in a private home, as it often does in Europe. Some San Franciscan 'Bed and Breakfast Inns' offer extremely lavish accommodation, and are often in restored Victorians with antique furnishings and a wealthy mansion feel. Examples are the Archbishop's Mansion on Alamo Square in Pacific Heights, the Artists Inn, Bed and Breakfast, and Inn 1890 in the Haight-Ashbury.

Apartments
If you want an apartment for a short-term holiday or business let there are specialist agencies you can contact. You can also stay in suite-only hotels where rooms have kitchen facilities, such as the Steinhart Hotel near Union Square. Renting an apartment in San Francisco for a long stay is best done once you're here – look in the newspaper advertisements and ask around. Prices for a room in shared accommodation are reasonable.

Rental Guide Magazine
2720 Taylor St. Tel: (415) 929 7777; www.rentalguide.com

Hostels
Hostels offer accommodation for all travellers, though their budget prices and communal facilities mean they are most popular with students and the young. Those belonging to the American Youth Hostel organisation (AYH; *www.hiayh.org*) are part of the worldwide youth hostelling network. Guests usually take their own sleeping bag.

Marin Headlands
Marin Headlands
Fort Barry, Building 941.
Tel: (415) 331 2777.
San Francisco City Center Hostel
685 Ellis St. Tel: (415) 474 5721.

San Francisco Downtown Hostel
312 Mason St at Union Square.
Tel: (415) 788 5604.
San Francisco Fisherman's Wharf Hostel
Dormitory accommodation in Civil War-era army barracks.
Fort Mason, Building 240.
Tel: (415) 771 7277.

Camping
There are no campsites in San Francisco city limits, but recreational camping is available in State Parks such as Angel Island, Mount Tamalpais and at Half Moon Bay.
General Information
California State Parks. www.parks.ca.gov
Reservations
ReserveAmerica. Tel: 800 444 7275 (toll-free); www.reserveamerica.com

The Bay Area has plenty of motels where you can spend an inexpensive night while touring

On business

A major commercial, financial and tourist centre, San Francisco is a progressive city where business and leisure are easily combined. It is regularly used for conventions by companies and institutions.

Flower seller in the
Financial District

Banks
Normally open Monday to Friday
9am–4pm, with some offering extended
hours on Fridays and Saturday
mornings. Money can also be changed
in major hotels. Take your passport or
some form of photo identification.
ATMs are 24-hour.

Business hours
Monday to Friday 9am–5pm, but many
business people start work earlier.

Business services
Ideas Unlimited (concierge services)
Tel: (415) 668 7089; www.iuui.com
Interpreters Unlimited
Tel: (800) 821 9999.
Mail Boxes Etc (packaging and
shipping) *268 Bush St.*
Tel: (415) 765 1515; www.mbe.com
Selix Formalwear
123 Kearny St.
Tel: (800) 735 4988, (415) 362 1133;
www.selix.com
Somewhere in Time (florists)
699 Folsom St. Tel: (800) 726 4909,
www.sitflowers.com

Courier services
FedEx (air courier)
1155 Harrison St. Tel: (800) 463 3339;
www.fedex.com

Special T Delivery (messenger service)
PO Box 422127. Tel: 415 357 9000.

Conference and exhibition facilities
Cow Palace
Multipurpose venue on southern city
limit used for trade shows, music, sport
and entertainment.
Geneva Ave and Santos St.
Tel: (415) 404 4100; www.cowpalace.com

Moscone Convention Center
Part of the Yerba Buena Gardens
complex (*see p97*); Moscone West is at
4th and Howard Sts.
744 Howard St. Tel: (415) 974 4000;
www.moscone.com

Dress
Look good but don't get hung up about
it – a sartorial philosophy borne out by
the many businesswomen who arrive
every morning by commuter ferry
sporting power suits and trainers, the
latter being swapped for chic heels left
in the office drawer. Suits and ties are
still the norm in the Financial District
and business-orientated restaurants, but
the rest of the city has gone more casual.

Etiquette
Californians express their enthusiasm
and positive feelings without fear,

and may misinterpret traditional European reserve as a negative reaction. They often turn up early for appointments – and if they arrive on time you can bet they'll apologise for being late, and blame it on traffic or transportation woes.

Lunch is a central part of business life and a prime reason for San Francisco's gastronomic vitality. If you are the host don't be afraid to ask your guests to suggest a few possible restaurants they might like to try. Business colleagues may well invite you to their homes or to social activities in the evening or at weekends – it's all part of the West Coast good life where work and play never cease.

Hotels

With so many San Francisco hotels competing for business travellers there are always new services and incentives to entice you here rather than there – perhaps a complimentary morning limousine to the Financial District, access to club-class floors, free family accommodation. If you have the time, it will pay to shop around.

All large hotels will have a conference room and currency exchange, and be able to book car hire, restaurants and excursions. Hotels and their restaurants are often used as venues for meetings, and many have business floors, satellite TV, business centres and audiovisual equipment. More and more are offering in-room fax, computer links, and high-speed and/or wireless Internet connections.

Media

San Francisco Business Times covers the Bay Area scene each week, and constantly updates its online version.
Tel: (415) 989 2522;
www.bizjournals.com/sanfrancisco

Travel arrangements
Fugazi Travel
600 Beach St, 3rd Floor. Tel: (800) 544 8728, (415) 397 7111;
www.fugazitravel.com

You've made it when they send a stretch limo

Practical guide

Arriving
Documents

All travellers must be in possession of a valid machine-readable passport. British and Australian citizens arriving by air are normally granted a visa waiver, but will need a visa if arriving in the US by other means. To travel visa-free your passport must be machine readable (and satisfy criteria detailed at *www.usembassy.org.uk* or *www.cbp.gov*). Citizens of South Africa require visas, which should be obtained in your country of residence. Visas are free and last the life of your passport. American immigration laws are strict, passport technology changes are ongoing, and should you have any queries consult your nearest US Consulate before departure. (*See also* Health and insurance *p180.*)

CalTrain rail station, the terminus for services south to San Jose, and Gilroy, 32km (20 miles) farther south

By air

San Francisco International Airport is 23km (14 miles) south of the city centre in San Bruno. There are also international airports at Oakland and San Jose.

Airport facilities

San Francisco International Airport (SFO) has four AirTrain-linked terminals: International and Terminals 1, 2 and 3. All four are linked by rail and road with a Bay Area Rapid Transit (BART) station at the International Terminal.

Departures are from the upper level and Arrivals on the lower. The airport has a full range of services including shops, museum, car hire (rental), hotel booking services and tourist information booths in the Arrivals halls.

Airport information
Tel: (650) 821 8211; www.flysfo.com
Parking information
Tel: (650) 821 7900.
Public transit information
Tel: 511 (Bay Area only); www.511.org
Airport transfers
Airporter buses (*www.flysfo.com*) serve the Bay Area *except* San Francisco. Private shuttle buses and vans depart from both upper levels and take passengers to wherever they are staying. The journey to the city centre takes about half an hour, longer in rush hour.
Quake City Shuttle
Tel: (415) 255 4899;
www.quakecityshuttle.com
SuperShuttle
Tel: (415) 558 8500, (650) 558 8500;
www.supershuttle.com

SamTrans

Tel: 511 or (800) 660 4287. Bus services KX, 292 and 397 connect SFO to the Transbay Terminal in downtown San Francisco (SOMA).

By coach

The Greyhound Bus runs services between San Francisco and numerous destinations. The cheap, slow and alternative Green Tortoise travels similar routes. Coaches depart from the Transbay Terminal at 425 Mission Street. (*Also see p183.*)

Greyhound Lines

Tel: (415) 495 1569 or *(800) 231 2222;* *www.greyhound.com*

Green Tortoise

Tel: (415) 956 7500 or *(800) 867 8647;* *www.greentortoise.com*

By rail

Amtrak rail services connect San Francisco with Los Angeles, Seattle and Chicago. A bus service from the Transbay Terminal connects at Oakland with the main coast line. There is a ticket office at the Transbay Terminal, 425 Mission Street.

Amtrak Information

Tel: (800) 872 7245; www.amtrak.com

The city's CalTrain (*www.caltrain.com*) railway station is at 700 Fourth Street at Townsend Street, and is the terminus for services operated by CalTrain to San Jose and beyond (*see p186*).

The bi-monthly *Thomas Cook Overseas Timetable* gives details of many rail, long-distance bus and shipping services in the US. You can buy it in the UK from some stations, online at *www.thomascookpublishing.com*, from

any office of Thomas Cook, or by telephoning *(01733) 416477.*

In the US contact: SF Travel Publications, 3959 Electric Road, Suite 155, Roanoke, VA 24018 (*tel: (800) 322 3834; www.travelbookstore.com*).

By road

From the south, Highway 1 is the most scenic route from Los Angeles, with the parallel US 101 a faster inland alternative. From the north, US 101 runs south from the Canadian border to cross the Golden Gate Bridge, and Interstate 80 runs southwest from Sacramento over the Bay Bridge.

By sea

San Francisco is frequently included in the itineraries of cruise ships – a good travel agent can supply up-to-date details. Ships shall dock at Pier 35 until a new cruise ship terminal debuts at Piers 30–32 in 2008.

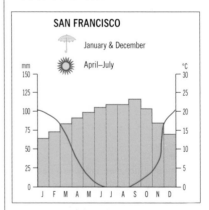

SAN FRANCISCO

January & December

April–July

mm
150
125
100
75
50
25
0
J F M A M J J A S O N D

°C
30
25
20
15
10
5
0

Weather Conversion Chart
25.4mm = 1 inch
°F = 1.8 x °C + 32

Climate

San Francisco is a year-round holiday
destination, but its summer fog creates
an idiosyncratic climate that can produce
many weathers in a single day. Winters
are often wet, summers always markedly
cooler than the rest of California.
Temperatures rarely fall below 5°C
(40°F) or rise above 21°C (70°F).

Consulates

Australia *575 Market Street, San
Francisco, CA 94105. Tel: (415) 536 1970.*
Canada *580 California Street, 14 Fl, San
Francisco, CA 94104. Tel: (415) 834 3180.*
Germany *1960 Jackson St, San
Francisco, CA 94109.
Tel: (415) 775 1061.*
Ireland *100 Pine Street, 33 Fl, San
Francisco, CA 94111. Tel: (415) 392
4214.*
New Zealand *One Maritime Plaza, Suite
700, San Francisco, CA 94111.
Tel: (415) 399 1255.*
United Kingdom *1 Sansome Street,
Suite 850, San Francisco, CA 94104.
Tel: (415) 617 1300.*

Conversion tables

Imperial measurements are used in
America. The only difference from their
UK equivalents is that gallon, quart and
pint measures are 20 per cent less.

Crime

Like many cities, San Francisco has its
crime problem. Common-sense
precautions can help ensure a trouble-
free visit, such as always using hotel
safe-deposit boxes, never carrying more
money than necessary (use credit cards
and refundable travellers' cheques rather
than cash), and avoiding confrontational
situations on the street.

The risk of crime is greatest at night:
never walk alone down dark or deserted
streets. Areas to avoid in particular are
the Tenderloin, Western Addition,
Potrero, and sections of the Mission and
SOMA. If you are going to a restaurant
or venue in these areas, take a cab both
ways. Don't hang around on the street
expecting one to pass – get someone to
call a cab company when you want to
leave. If you hire a car, leave no valuables
inside and never give lifts to hitchhikers.

Customs regulations

The most common customs regulation
met by visitors to the United States is
the absolute ban on importing fresh
fruit, meat, cheese, plants, seeds, and
unprocessed agricultural products. All
visitors are required to fill in a customs
declaration form on arrival. Medication
available over the counter abroad, which
is prescription-only in the US, may be
confiscated by US customs officials
unless you have a doctor's certificate.
Duty-free allowances for travellers over 21
entering the country are 1 litre of alcohol/
spirits, 200 cigarettes or 50 cigars (not
Cuban) and $100-worth of gifts.
*www.cbp.gov/linkhandler/cgov/toolbox/
publications/travel/visitingtheunitedstates.
ctt/visitingtheunitedstates.doc*

Dress

Take clothes for spring-like weather, and
bear in mind that it can be cold on the
ferries and Golden Gate Bridge, and
even colder when the fogs of summer
roll in. San Francisco benefits from a
constant breeze that can create a wind-

chill factor in lower temperatures. Most Californians like to dress smart but casual in layers – a few top restaurants expect men to wear a jacket and tie.

Driving
Car rental
If you are visiting on a package holiday, try to arrange car rental before you leave home, but be aware that seemingly unavoidable add-on charges can virtually double your original bill. Check the figures before you pay, and demand explanations if necessary. All bills are subject to 8.5 per cent sales tax in San Francisco; slightly lower elsewhere.

Drivers must hold a valid driving licence and be over 21. Most car hire companies require that all drivers be at least 25 years old. You will also need a credit card to provide a deposit, though some companies may accept a substantial cash amount instead. All hire cars have automatic gears – if you are unfamiliar with these ask for a few minutes instruction before hitting the road. Petrol in the US is cheap by European standards, and virtually all hire cars take unleaded or diesel. Petrol stations are not as common as you might expect, so fill up before you set off for, say, Point Reyes National Seashore. Car hire rates are cheapest at airports and more expensive from city locations. The following telephone numbers are toll-free:

Alamo
320 O'Farrell St. Tel: 800 327 9633. www.alamo.com
Avis
675 Post St. Tel: 800 831 2847. www.avis.com

Conversion Table

FROM	TO	MULTIPLY BY
Inches	Centimetres	2.54
Feet	Metres	0.3048
Yards	Metres	0.9144
Miles	Kilometres	1.6090
Acres	Hectares	0.4047
Gallons	Litres	4.5460
Ounces	Grams	28.35
Pounds	Grams	453.6
Pounds	Kilograms	0.4536
Tons	Tonnes	1.0160

To convert back, for example from centimetres to inches, divide by the number in the third column.

Men's Suits

UK		36	38	40	42	44	46	48
Rest of Europe	46	48	50	52	54	56	58
USA		36	38	40	42	44	46	48

Dress Sizes

UK		8	10	12	14	16	18
France		36	38	40	42	44	46
Italy		38	40	42	44	46	48
Rest of Europe	34	36	38	40	42	44
USA		6	8	10	12	14	16

Men's Shirts

UK	14	14.5	15	15.5	16	16.5	17
Rest of Europe	36	37	38	39/40	41	42	43
USA	14	14.5	15	15.5	16	16.5	17

Men's Shoes

UK		7	7.5	8.5	9.5	10.5	11
Rest of Europe	41	42	43	44	45	46
USA		8	8.5	9.5	10.5	11.5	12

Women's Shoes

UK		4.5	5	5.5	6	6.5	7
Rest of Europe	38	38	39	39	40	41
USA		6	6.5	7	7.5	8	8.5

Budget Rent-a-Car
321 Mason St. Tel: 800 527 7000.
www.budget.com
Dollar
364 O'Farrell St. Tel: 800 800 4000.
www.dollar.com
Hertz
433 Mason St. Tel: 800 704 4473.
www.hertz.com

On the road
Drive on the right. The maximum speed limit is 55 miles per hour (88 kph) on highways and 25 miles per hour (40 kph) unless posted otherwise. Seat belts are compulsory in front seats. San Francisco's grid of streets includes steep hills and a convoluted one-way system – remember that cable cars have right of way. There is a toll for drivers coming south across the Golden Gate Bridge and west across the Bay Bridge.
Local transportation and traffic information *tel: 511. www.511.org*

Parking
Parking restrictions are enforced with vigour. Look up to check signs detailing street-cleaning times and tow-away zones, then down for the colour of the curb. Anywhere painted red, yellow, yellow-and-black, yellow-and-black-and-green, blue (unless you are a disabled driver), white and green (unless you are stopping five or 10 minutes respectively) are out. If you find anything in between all this, grab it!
San Francisco has many off-street and multistorey car parks that advertise their prices with loud signs, or you can chance your luck finding a meter in the street. 'Valet Parking', where hotels and restaurants charge to park your car for you, is common, and many shopping centres offer 'Validated Parking', where parking is free or discounted if you show a purchase receipt on departure.
When parking on the city's steep hills, you are required by law to turn your vehicle's front wheels into the curb facing downhill, to the street facing uphill. Don't forget the handbrake.

Electricity
Standard electrical supply in the US is 110 volts (60 cycles). Sockets take flat two-pin plugs, so UK and European appliances will need an adaptor.

Emergency telephone numbers
Dial *911* for **Police**, **Fire** and **Ambulance** services.

Health and insurance
There are no mandatory vaccination requirements for entering the US, but tetanus and polio immunisation should be kept up to date, and other international health precautions should be observed. As in many parts of the world, AIDS is present. The latest health advice can be obtained from the US Centers for Disease Control and Prevention (CDC).
www.cdc.gov

If you need to consult a doctor or dentist, ask at your hotel or look in the *Yellow Pages* telephone directory.
Saint Francis Memorial Hospital
900 Hyde St. Tel: (415) 353 6000.
www.saintfrancismemorial.org

San Francisco General Hospital
1001 Potrero Ave. Tel: (415) 206 8000.
www.dph-sf.ca-us/chn/SFGH
San Francisco Dental Office
131 Steuart St, Suite 323.
Tel: (415) 777 5115.

Chemists

Drugstores are a common feature of San Francisco's streets and sell a multitude of self-help medications. Most have a pharmacist on duty who can dispense prescriptions.
Walgreen's is open 24 hours (*498 Castro St, tel: (415) 861 3136. Also at 3201 Divisadero St, tel: (415) 931 6417*).

Insurance

Medical care in the US is very expensive. Adequate medical insurance is highly recommended, and is a pre-travel requirement with many package holidays.

Lost property

If you lose anything of value inform the police, if only for insurance purposes. The loss of a passport should be reported to your consulate immediately.
MUNI Lost and Found (public transport) *Tel: (415) 923 6168, or 511; www.sfmuni.com*

Maps

Free city maps are available from the San Francisco Visitor Information Center (*see p23*). Rand McNally (*www.randmcnally.com*) publish several useful maps of the Bay Area. For Napa and Sonoma Wine Country Touring, check *www.winecountry.com*

Media
Newspapers and magazines

The city has one comprehensive daily paper: the morning *San Francisco Chronicle* (*www.sfgate.com*). On Sunday, it balloons to a wrist-wearying tome that can number more than a dozen sections. Useful supplements include the Wednesday Food and Thursday Wine sections and the pink Sunday *Datebook* that contains the latest what's on listings.

The free tabloid *San Francisco Examiner* is published six times a week (*www.examiner.com*).

Free weekly papers dispensed from kerbside lockers at major commuter points provide helpful and absorbing reading. The weekly San Francisco Bay *Guardian* (*www.sfbg.com*) and *SF Weekly* (*www.sfweekly.com*) are bibles of San Francisco's alternative scene and the best source of offbeat poetry readings, live music and nightlife. Numerous monthly magazines, like *San Francisco Magazine* (*www.sanfran.com*), *7x7* and *Bay City* (*www.baycityguide.com*), are pitched at visiting tourists and also contain cultural listings.

TV and radio

Don't stay in to watch American television, which has countless channels but little essential viewing. If you want to relax, many hotels have videos or DVDs for hire of films starring San Francisco. The choice of radio stations is even more prolific, and you can usually find something to while away the traffic jams or underscore a scenic drive. Start your sampling with some jazz, country and western, classical, '70s classics, hip-hop, rock 'n' roll, or a range of Spanish-language offerings. News and chat are carried on the AM band by stations like KCBS (740 AM) and KGO (810 AM).

Money matters

Currency

The American unit of currency is the dollar ($), divided into 100 cents (¢) Banknotes are issued for 1 (a buck), 2, 5, 10, 20, 50 and 100 dollars; coins for 1 (a penny), 5 (a nickel), 10 (a dime), 25 (a quarter) and 50 cents. All banknotes are printed the same size and with minor colour variation, so be vigilant. Keep a stock of quarters for parking meters and other coin-operated machines.

Travellers' cheques

Travellers' cheques avoid the hazards of carrying large amounts of cash, and can be quickly refunded in the event of their loss or theft. Travellers' cheques must be denominated in US dollars, and are widely accepted in lieu of cash.

Credit cards

Credit cards are so widely used in America that travel can become difficult if you do not own at least one in a major name. A card imprint or swipe will normally be taken when you hire a car or check into a hotel, and in some cases, such as when you rent a bicycle or drink at an upmarket bar, you will be asked to surrender the card until you settle your bill later. Debit cards that deduct directly from a bank account are also popular.

Taxes

Taxes vary from state to state in the US. In San Francisco, there is an 8.5 per cent sales tax on all purchases except food for preparation and prescription drugs. Other counties have different tax rates, but the difference will be minor. Hotel bills in the city are subject to a 14 per cent transient tax. There is no airport or departure tax; airport taxes are included in the price of airline tickets.

Opening times

Banks are open at least Monday to Friday 9am–4pm (*see p174*). For shops *see p138*. The favoured closing day for museums is Monday.

Places of worship

Many religions, both old and new, have places of worship in San Francisco. Ask at your hotel or the San Francisco Visitor Information Center for locations and service times.

See also entries for Grace Cathedral, St Mary's Cathedral and Old St Mary's Church (Chinatown).

Police

Police wear dark blue uniforms, carry arms and are there to help.
Emergency *Tel: 911.*
Non-emergency *Tel: (415) 553 0123.*

Post offices

Post offices are usually open Monday to Friday 9am–5pm and Saturday 9am–1pm, but times vary with location. The most aesthetic venue to carry out transactions is amid the 1940s murals of the Rincon Center (*see p139*). Stamps can also be bought from most hotels, vending machines and some grocery stores and shops. Mail boxes are dark blue and often have only one collection a day.

Letters should be sent to your hotel or, if necessary, to 'General Delivery' and addressed to the nearest post office. For post office addresses and zip codes, consult the United States Postal Service *www.usps.com*

Public holidays

1 January New Year's Day
January, 3rd Monday Martin Luther King Jr Day
February, 3rd Monday President's Day
Variable Easter Sunday and Monday
May, Last Monday Memorial Day
4 July Independence Day
September, 1st Monday Labor Day
October, 2nd Monday Columbus Day
11 November Veteran's Day
November, 4th Thursday Thanksgiving Day
25 December Christmas Day

Public transport

Public transport in San Francisco is operated by MUNI, who produce free timetables and an inexpensive *Street and Transit Map* listing all routes and connections, available from Metro stations, MUNI kiosks and some bookstores.

You can find a MUNI map online at *http://transit.511.org/providers/maps/ SF_915200524737.gif*

Discount fares apply if 65 or over or under 18. Under-fives travel free. For details of MUNI Passports, and for taxis, see p21. For ferries see p130.
MUNI information
Tel: (415) 673 6864; www.sfmuni.com
General transport and traffic information
Tel: 511; www.511.org

Bus
Bus stops are indicated by an orange MUNI sign or a yellow stripe on lampposts. Board at the front and exit at the rear. There is a flat fare of $1.50. Show your pass or pay cash as you enter (drivers give no change) and take a transfer from the driver – you must have

May the law be with you: San Francisco policeman

proof of payment at all times or risk a substantial fine. Transfers also allow you trips (except cable cars) within the time period shown, at least 90 minutes. When getting off, step down to the door to make it open automatically.

Metro

MUNI operates six streetcar routes that combine subway and surface travel, each designated by letters from J to N, plus F (with historic streetcars). Buy tickets from machines in Metro stations or on board if above ground.

Cable cars

There are three lines – look carefully at the painted signs on the cars to get the right route. Stops are marked by brown signs with a cable car picture. Tickets cost $5 with no transfers permitted. The crew have designated areas that have to be kept clear, marked by yellow lines on the floor – if you stand in them, expect to hear about it. *See pp24–5.*

BART

The four lines of the Bay Area Rapid Transit (BART) District link cities in four counties around the Bay Area as well as Oakland and San Francisco International Airports. Tickets are bought from station machines – you can add to their value later. Trains carry the name of their final destination.
BART Information *Tel: (415) 989 2278; www.bart.gov*

Bay Area

To take advantage of the Bay Area public transport, get the inexpensive *San Francisco Bay Area Regional Transit Guide*

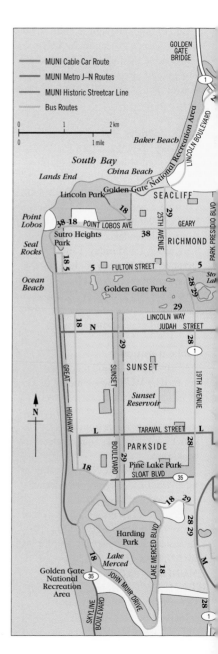

MUNI and BART transport

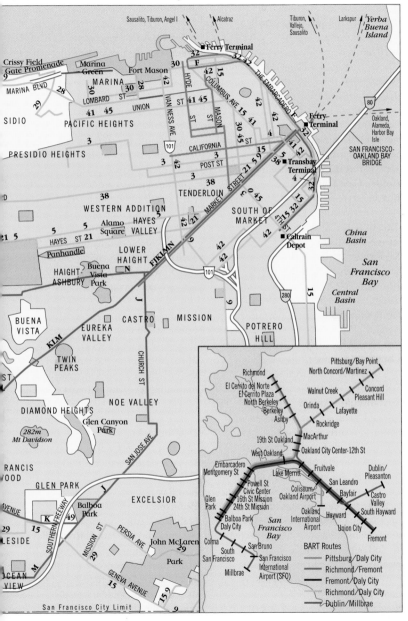

Sausalito, Tiburon, Angel I   Alcatraz   Tiburon,   Larkspur   *Yerba
                                               Vallejo,   *Buena
                                               Sausalito   *Island*

Ferry Terminal

Crissy Field
Gate Promenade   Marina
9   Green   Fort Mason   F
                                                                Ferry
MARINA   Terminal
MARINA BLVD   28   Oakland,
                  30   30   28   Alameda,
            LOMBARD   ST   Harbor Bay
PACIFIC HEIGHTS   UNION   Isle
         41   45   SAN FRANCISCO-
SIDIO   OAKLAND BAY
                                                                BRIDGE
PRESIDIO HEIGHTS   3
              3   CALIFORNIA
         3   Transbay
            3   POST ST   Terminal
         3   38
              38   TENDERLOIN   SOUTH OF
WESTERN ADDITION   MARKET
         5   5   Alamo   HAYES   *China*
21 5   Square   VALLEY   *Basin*
        HAYES ST 21   *San*
            Panhandle   *Francisco*
              LOWER   Caltrain   *Bay*
              HAIGHT   Depot
HAIGHT-   Buena   *Central*
ASHBURY   Vista   N   *Basin*
           Park
BUENA
VISTA   EUREKA
             VALLEY
      TWIN
      PEAKS
                CASTRO   MISSION
                                    POTRERO
                                    HILL
DIAMOND HEIGHTS
        282m   Glen Canyon
       Mt Davidson Park
                              Pittsburg/Bay Point
                     Richmond   North Concord/Martinez
              El Cerrito del Norte
              El Cerrito Plaza   Walnut Creek   Concord
              North Berkeley   Orinda   Pleasant Hill
                  Berkeley
                  Ashby   Lafayette
RANCIS   Rockridge
WOOD   19th St Oakland   MacArthur
    GLEN PARK   West Oakland   Oakland City Center-12th St
                 Embarcadero
                 Montgomery St   Lake Merritt   Fruitvale   Dublin/
                     Powell St   Pleasanton
                     Civic Center Coliseum/ San Leandro
              Glen   16th St Mission Oakland Airport Bayfair Castro
              Park   24th St Mission   Valley
EXCELSIOR   Balboa Park   Hayward South Hayward
                  Daly City   *San*   Oakland
                             Francisco International Union City
                  Colma   *Bay*   Airport   Fremont
29   15   South   BART Routes
LESIDE   San Francisco San Bruno
                  Millbrae   San Francisco   Pittsburg/Daly City
                             International   Richmond/Fremont
OCEAN   Airport (SFO)   Fremont/Daly City
VIEW   Richmond/Daly City
       San Francisco City Limit   Dublin/Millbrae

published by the Metropolitan
Transport Commission, available
from bookstores.

AC Transit
Bus services to Berkeley, Oakland and
the East Bay.
Tel: 511 or 817 1717.
www.octransit.org

CalTrain
Rail services between San Francisco and
San Jose, south to Gilroy.
Tel: (800) 660 4287; www.caltrain.com

Golden Gate Transit
Bus and ferry services to Contra Costa
Marin and Sonoma Counties.
Tel: (415) 455 2000;
www.goldengatetransit.org

SamTrans
Bus services in San Mateo County to
Palo Alto.
Tel: (800) 660 4287; www.samtrans.com

**Santa Clara Valley Transportation
Agency**
Bus services in San Jose and Santa Clara
County, to Fremont.
Tel: (800) 894 9908; www.vta.org

Sustainable tourism

Thomas Cook is a strong advocate of
ethical and fairly traded tourism and
believes that the travel experience should
be as good for the places visited as it is for
the people who visit them. That's why we
firmly support The Travel Foundation,
a charity that develops solutions to help
improve and protect holiday destinations,
their environment, traditions and culture.
To find out what you can do to make a
positive difference to the places you
travel to and the people who live
there, please visit
www.thetravelfoundation.org.uk

Telephones

Local telephone calls are cheap, and
phonecards may be cheaper, so treat the
phone as a sightseeing tool that can be
used for checking opening times and
transport arrangements, and for making
reservations for shows and restaurants.

The rates charged by hotels for calls
from your room and internet
connections vary considerably – check
the tariffs before you dial to avoid a
shock on departure.

Some numbers are advertised with
easy-to-remember letters replacing the
last four digits, such as *415 673 MUNI*.
Look for the letter on the phone and
dial the corresponding number. Those
prefixed *1 800, 888, 877 or 866* are toll-
free. Reverse charge calls, arranged
through the operator, are called 'collect'.

Payphones

Public telephones take 5, 10 and 25 cent
coins, and some accept credit cards.
Most bars have a payphone too. As the
use of cellular phones increases, it is
becoming very hard to find a working
public pay phone.

Dialling codes

The area code for San Francisco is *415*.
If you are calling from within the city
you do not need to use it. Area codes:
East Bay *510 & 925*
Peninsula (just south of San
Francisco) *650*
San Jose and much of Silicon Valley *408*

To call-long distance within the US,
dial 1 then the area code and number.
To call abroad from the US, dial *011*,
then the country code, then the
number omitting any initial 0.

Some international codes are:

Australia *61*
France *33*
Germany *49*
Irish Republic *353*
Mexico *52*
New Zealand *64*
South Africa *27*
UK *44*
No code is necessary to call Canada from the US.

Operator *0*
Directory Enquiries local *411*
Directory Enquiries for long-distance dial *1* then area code then *555 1212*.

Time

California is in the Pacific Standard Time zone, which is 8 hours behind GMT. When it is noon in San Francisco it is 3pm in New York and 8pm in London. The clocks are put forward one hour from the first Sunday in April to the first Sunday in October. For the exact time, *tel: 767 2676 (POP-CORN)*.

Tipping

Tipping is expected in America, but do as you feel the service merits. Suitable amounts are $1 a bag for a porter, 15 per cent for taxis and 15–20 per cent in restaurants and bars.

Toilets

Public toilets are commonly known as Rest Rooms, sometimes Bathrooms.

Tourist information

Overseas

For information on San Francisco before you leave home, there are US Tourist Offices in many cities around the world. A few are devoted specifically to California, including:

Germany, Austria & Switzerland
MSI
Frankfurter Strasse 175
63263 Neu Isenberg, Germany.
Tel: 61 02 207 946.

Have a great time – this is classic San Francisco

UK

McCluskey and Associates
4 Vencourt Place,
Hammersmith, London W6 9WV.
Tel: 0208 237 7979.

California

The official state Visitor's Guide and
travel planner are online.
California Tourism, PO Box 1499,
Sacramento, CA 95812-1499.
Tel: (800) 462 2543, (916) 444 4429;
info@cttc1.com; www.visitcalifornia.com

San Francisco

See p23. www.onlyinsanfrancisco.com
offers lots of information. Postal
enquiries to *San Francisco Convention &*
Visitors Bureau, 201 Third St, Suite 900,
San Francisco CA 94103-3185.
See individual entries for tourist offices
in the Bay Area.

Travellers with disabilities

San Francisco is one of the
most accessible cities in the
world for disabled visitors.
Most transport services,
including airport shuttle
buses, MUNI buses and
BART stations and trains,
have facilities for wheelchairs,
and public buildings must
have purpose-built access.
Information on services for
the disabled is available by
telephone (numbers prefixed
TDD are for users with
impaired hearing).
   Access San Francisco is a
guide to all services, for
download at

http://onlysf.sfvisitor.org/plan_your_trip/
access_guide.asp, a site with other links
for transportation and parking. Find
Northern California information at
www.accessnca.com

Information

Mayor's Office on Disability *401 Van*
Ness Ave, Room 300, San Francisco CA
94102.
Tel: (415) 554 6789, TY: (415) 554 6799;
www.sfgov.org/sfmod
MUNI Accessible Service Programs
(public transport)
1 South Van Ness Ave, Fl.3, San Francisco
CA 94103-1267.
Tel: (415) 701 4485;
www.sfmuni.com/access
San Francisco Convention & Visitors
Bureau TTD/TTY
Tel: (415) 392 0328.
Easter Seal Society (information)
Tel: (415) 744 8754;
www.easter-seals.org

Flags line the façade of The Fairmont San Francisco hotel atop
Nob Hill

ACKNOWLEDGEMENTS
Thomas Cook Publishing wishes to thank the following libraries and associations for their assistance in the preparation of this book, and to whom the copyright in the photographs belongs.

FRED GEBHART 7, 12

MAXINE CASS 4, 8, 14b, 17, 22, 23, 24, 25a, 25b, 26, 33a, 33b, 34a, 37, 39a, 40, 41, 42b, 43a, 43b, 44, 45, 47, 48, 51, 54, 59, 61, 62, 63, 67, 68a, 70a, 73, 74, 75, 78, 87, 89, 90, 91, 94, 95a, 96, 97, 99, 103, 106, 108, 110, 112, 113, 114, 117, 121a, 122, 123, 133, 134, 135, 137b, 141, 143, 146, 147a, 147b, 149, 150, 151, 158, 160, 161a, 161b, 162, 164, 166, 167a, 167b, 170, 171b, 174, 176, 187, 188

MARY EVANS PICTURE LIBRARY 13a, 13b

NEIL SETCHFIELD 137a

REX FEATURES 68b, 69

SAN FRANCISCO CONVENTION & VISITORS BUREAU 56 (TOM BROSS), 57a (CRAIG BUCHANAN), 57b (PHIL COBLENTZ), 152 (JACK HOLLINGSWORTH)

The remaining pictures are held in the AA PHOTO LIBRARY and were taken by KEN PATERSON.

Index: MARIE LORIMER

Proofreading: JAN McCANN FOR CAMBRIDGE PUBLISHING MANAGEMENT LIMITED

Send your thoughts to
books@thomascook.com

We're committed to providing the very best up-to-date information in our travel guides and constantly strive to make them as useful as they can be. You can help us to improve future editions by letting us have your feedback. If you've made a wonderful discovery on your travels that we don't already feature, if you'd like to inform us about recent changes to anything that we do include, or if you simply want to let us know your thoughts about this guidebook and how we can make it even better – we'd love to hear from you.

Send us ideas, discoveries and recommendations today and then look out for your valuable input in the next edition of this title. And, as an extra 'thank you' from Thomas Cook Publishing, you'll be automatically entered into our exciting monthly prize draw.

Emails to the above address, or letters to Travellers Project Editor, Thomas Cook Publishing, PO Box 227, Unit 18, Coningsby Road, Peterborough PE3 8SB, UK.

Please don't forget to let us know which title your feedback refers to!